IT'S NOT BLOODY ROCKET SCIENCE...

Dulcie Shepherd Swanston is the owner of Profitably Engaged, an Executive Coaching Company, the founder of Tea Break Training and spent over 20 years in leadership roles across Operations and Human Resources for a FTSE 250 company. Her work has been cited in the Sunday Telegraph and on BBC Radio 5 Live and she believes herself to be the only Fellow of the CIPD who is also a qualified nightclub bouncer. She lives in Warwickshire with her husband, two dogs and between one and five of their children.

Visit her online at www.profitablyengaged.com

Also available as an e Book.

For Lyra, Amelie, Amelia, Alex, Emma and Jamie
– my amazing table for seven

Dulcie has the uncanny knack of making what should be boring theory actually mean something. Better than that, you can actually use her interpretation in real life and it works...!

JAMES PAVEY. *Operations Director.*
Tesco Hospitality

Hallelujah! It might not be rocket science but as a scientist, this book does contains real science I recognise and not celebrity pseudoscience about vitamins and hair... Dulcie has used it to produce a down to earth and genuinely useful handbook which is based on logic and everyday evidence we will all recognise.

SARRA LAYCOCK. *Chief Operating Officer.*
Sequani (Pharmaceuticals) Ltd

This is a great read, as usual, Dulcie makes us think about the way we approach getting things done. Like her, it is a great mix of the practical and well researched.

DENNIS DEARE. *Brand Operations Director.*
Mitchells and Butlers

Dulcie is one of the most perceptive people I have ever worked with and has an amazing ability to turn my jumbled thoughts into usable leadership actions. This book will do the same for you... she is a bloody superstar!

MATT SNELL. *Managing Director.*
Gusto Restaurants

Dulcie is one of those people that cuts through crap faster than the speed of light. In this book, she unpicks all of those wicked problems we face as leaders and tackles them with fearlessness, courage and kick-ass. If you want a no-nonsense approach to just about everything to do with leadership, read this book!

KADISHA LEWIS-ROBERTS. *HR Director. Talent and Operations. AFEMEA. Amcor*

It's a leadership book, but not as we know it. Dulcie exemplifies the blend of warmth, courage and straight talking honesty that leaders need to grow and these qualities bounce off her pages. If you want genuine change in your personal or professional life, you will think Dulcie is a star. If you are just pretending, I'd keep to the opposite side of the planet.

DR CHRIS EDGER. *Professor of Multi-Unit Leadership, Birmingham City University Business School*

She is a straight talking Yorkshire woman who is pretty brutal with her knowledge of science, research and real-life experience. It doesn't leave you much room for making excuses not to challenge yourself. So you probably shouldn't read this if you secretly want to stay doing exactly what you have always done...

MARK MILLET. *Managing Director. Chef and Brewer Restaurants*

I always remember a conversation with Dulcie where I honestly stated "I don't quite know what to do" – she smiled and carefully asked "If you did know what to do, what do you think it would be?" Without realising, I replied with an idea that I didn't even know I had! – I still use this question with my own team members today – with great results. This book will do the same for you – provide you with insight and understanding that you will actually remember and use with real benefits.

MARTYN ALLEN. *Distribution Manager – UK and Ireland.*
Parker Ltd

My father was actually a rocket scientist! So I have been flippantly using this well-known expression throughout my career.

Dulcie has given it an extra dimension, challenging the comfortable day to day approach many of us stick to in order to lead. She helps us unlock our potential to be infinitely better .... and beyond ......?!

JAMES SILVERTHORNE. *Production Director.*
St George Developments Limited

IT'S NOT BLOODY ROCKET SCIENCE...

Life and Leadership Hacks
via Psychology, Neuroscience
and Common Sense

Dulcie Swanston

First published in 2019 by
Top Right Thinking Limited

Copyright © Dulcie Shepherd Swanston

The right of Dulcie Shepherd Swanston to be identified as the
author of this work has been asserted by her in accordance
with the Copyright, Design and Patents Act 1988.

Designed by Couper Street Type Co.

ISBN 978-1-9160853-0-5

CONTENTS

INTRODUCTION

Let me put my cards on the table (it's that sort of book). Whilst I have more than twenty years' experience of leading people – mostly in a company turning over £2 billion per annum, and I now own and operate *Profitably Engaged*, an executive coaching company that helps organisations to recruit, train and develop their leaders, I'm not a qualified neuroscientist or a psychologist. I did look into whether there was some sort of way to get one of those T-shirts and become a 'proper' doctor. I spent a couple of months investigating how I might put my degree, an MBA, my Fellowship of the Chartered Institute of Personnel and Development and two other postgraduate qualifications towards a PhD that sounded official and convincing enough to reassure people I knew what I was talking about.

It was possible, but for once in my life I was realistic. With the time constraints of running two businesses of my own, working part time for another and trying to keep track of five children, two dogs and a husband whose head office was four hours from home, it wasn't practical to go back to school. So I put both the idea and the early draft of *It's Not Bloody Rocket Science* ... on hold. After all, who would want to read a book on neuroscience and psychology written by someone who was neither a neuroscientist nor a psychologist?

Well, apparently quite a few people ... My clients kept asking me if I was still writing 'the book' and told me that, if I wrote it, they would buy it. They were very encouraging and assured me that the way I describe the science, making it simple to understand and use in real life, works for them.

There are many, many books by doctors and professors that will take you through these concepts in a lot more detail than I provide. Some are excellent. I have quoted directly from several of my personal favourites here, and I hope you will feel motivated to investigate them in more detail.

However, I have noticed that, no matter how highly a work might be recommended – 'Have you read this, Dulcie, you'll love it, it's brilliant!' – people (myself included) would just jump from one book to the next without putting into practice any of the ideas they had just been reading about. The next book was usually 'brilliant' too, but despite ingesting all this wonderful theory, nothing we were *doing* at work seemed to be changing as a result. We were well read, but not much seemed to stick beyond using a couple of buzzwords now and again. We were investing a lot of time and enthusiasm reading about new ideas and theories, but less time thinking and talking about why any ideas that we had tried to implement at work hadn't lasted for more than a month or so.

We can be genuinely attracted to an idea from a book or training course and appreciate that it could, in time, be life-changing, but it is not always obvious how we can actually implement it RIGHT NOW – in real life. I know, from helping many people to grow their skills over more than twenty years, that juggling the demands of a new job, a heavy workload and a growing family leaves little time to be as well read as you'd like. In my experience, it is even harder to make room in your life to translate theory into practice.

This book aims to be different. I have tried to explain some really cool science and research well enough for you to understand it, but simply enough that you'll be able to remember it for more than a week or two. I've deliberately avoided depth and detail, trying instead to replicate on the page what works for my clients in the field – to keep the theory as simple as possible so you can spend less of your precious time reading and more of it actually using some of the practical suggestions. Most of the examples I give for translating the science and research into real life are tried and tested by people just like you. People with real jobs and a busy life.

I hope my practical experience is as much help to you as my qualifications and research. Before I became an executive coach and the founder of a training business, I spent many happy years managing large teams of people. I did this in very different environments – from looking after groups of pubs and nightclubs as an area manager to running large 'corporate' teams in a more conventional office setting. What I hope you recognise in this book is that I didn't then (and don't now) think I was 'perfect' or 'the finished article'. I point this out because understanding that I didn't have to be either of these things to become an effective leader was a real 'Doh' moment. Even after twenty-plus years of experience and reading, I was still hoping to find the 'secret' – the silver bullet that would make me a leader who knew everything. If I worked hard enough, I could have it all sorted and error-free, have a perfectly organised life and never say the wrong thing ever again. The realisation that striving to be perfect was holding me back was liberating.

I have discovered instead that it can be game-changing to admit, 'I haven't a clue to be honest, what do you think?', and that more can be achieved in the long run by having just one great conversation that gets someone to *really* use their brain than by getting twenty things on a 'to do' list sorted.

It is now my business, through coaching, training and mentoring, to encourage others to embrace their imperfect brains and their mistakes. I help people to use aspects of neuroscience and psychology in their real lives in order to understand areas of potential underperformance. By doing so they can not only unlock more potential than they believed themselves to have but also make their work and home lives a lot less stressful.

Each chapter contains a couple of key elements of scientific research that my clients have told me have made a genuine and lasting difference to their lives. I have read thousands of pages on how to become a better leader, a more efficient person and a more effective parent. I hope this book saves you having to do the same.

Almost everyone talks about being time poor, and I've written *It's Not Bloody Rocket Science* with that absolutely in mind. I'm hoping that a book that covers ten books' worth of ground in one book's worth of words will give you some room to put theory into practice and achieve some quick wins at work or at home that will actually save you some time overall.

You can then choose either to reinvest that saved time into becoming even more successful at whatever you choose to do, or to spend it pursuing a favourite pastime or having fun with friends and family.

That's the hope. Before we start, something I'm fond of telling people is:

> **Only a fool or a liar would say that they understand the human brain.**

I tell clients this to remove any concerns that they don't know enough about psychology or neuroscience to confidently use the ideas. We can't hope to know everything there is to know about the brain, but we do know enough to be getting on with.

I can't find an attribution of these words of wisdom on the internet, so I presume I made them up myself (if you know differently, please let me know). Regardless, I can credit some of the inspiration to John S. Allen, a research neuroscientist who wrote in *The Lives of the Brain*:

> **The human brain, via religion or science, art or technology, has yet to figure itself out.**

The psychoanalyst Stephen Grosz, who in his beautiful and clever book *The Examined Life* explores the experience of being human and fallible, reassures us that:

> It takes time – it took me time – to realise just how very different people are from each other.

And finally the oft quoted:

> If the human brain were so simple that we *could* understand it, we would be so simple that we couldn't.

This brain twisting thought is usually attributed to Emerson Pugh who was a physicist and professor at the Carnegie Institute of Technology.

These wise words help us to understand we would be liars if we said we completely understood our own motives or thoughts and foolish to assume we could understand anyone else's.

What we can do is work with what we have, and not worry about whether it's cutting-edge thinking or the 'final word'. We've got enough to be getting on with – so let's get on with doing something.

ABOUT THIS BOOK

Here is a summary of what the ten chapters cover. Although they are best read in order, as some of them build on the science from earlier chapters, it's by no means essential, so if there is one topic in particular that grabs you, start there instead.

Chapter 1 – LIES – You aren't being honest with yourself. Don't worry. It's entirely normal

Once you understand how effective your brain is at lying (both to other people and to yourself), life can get really interesting with lots of new opportunities to grasp.

Chapter 2 – DON'T WORK HARDER – Think better

A tough one. If you regularly use 'I don't have time' as an excuse and think everyone should just buck their ideas up and work harder, your brain might strongly resist this chapter.

Chapter 3 – EVIDENCE – There is a slight problem with 'data', 'evidence' and 'proof'

This chapter may help you understand why you haven't been able to convince people to invest in your idea or do something they don't want to – even when you have all the 'facts'.

Chapter 4 – IMPOSTER! – Why you might be able to sleep better at night
Ever worried that the promotion you have just accepted is a step too far … that you are out of your depth and you are finally going to get found out? Don't worry – it's normal.

Chapter 5 – SCARF – How you could be dramatically reducing the performance of your people … without realising it
Our status, certainty, autonomy, relatedness and sense of fairness matter to us enormously. Sometimes other people underperforming might be more about you than them … Don't worry. It's fixable.

Chapter 6 – BE MORE LIKE ME – Why it's a good job that everyone is not 'a bit more like you'
Some good science about why the people you ought to recruit often give you the 'wrong' answers at interviews and will probably drive you mad.

Chapter 7 – LESS DOING, MORE THINKING – Short on time? Be smart about where you spend it
The power of reflection and working within our sphere of influence. Put more simply – stop, think and stick to your knitting.

Chapter 8 – CHANGE IS IMPOSSIBLE – Well almost …
Why, even though you know you can and should change, you will probably fail to do so. A bit depressing, but there is light at the end of the tunnel.

Chapter 9 – TOP RIGHT – The problem with leadership

Leadership is harder than it looks ... People strangely need to warm to you as a person AND see you as strong. At the same time. Damn! No wonder it's nearly impossible to pull off.

Chapter 10 – COACH – Coaching, mentoring, leading and managing – what works where and when?

Given the thousands of books written and the hoops you have to jump through to join a coaching body, you would think it really is rocket science. Erm, no. The principles are pretty easy to understand and you could start coaching and mentoring today. If not 'job done' then at least 'job started'.

To try to keep things simple and easy to follow, each chapter has the same structure:

The Big Idea

This is the science and research in a nutshell. To get the most out of the book, I would recommend finishing a chapter in one go and then immediately doing something as a result of what you read. Some Big Ideas are bigger than others and might take some time to get your head round, so I've indicated this at the outset by calling them Really Big Ideas. If you only have five minutes spare, it's probably better to tackle a Big Idea instead.

Got It – Now What?

These sections contain some practical suggestions for putting the theory into practice. Right now!

Top Right Questions

Chapter 9 explains exactly why I label great questions that offer people tough challenges phrased in a supportive way as 'Top Right' questions.

All I'll say for now is that these are questions you can ask yourself or other people that might help you to translate the science or research from the chapter into real-life practice.

Learn More and Share

In most chapters I have included sources of information for anyone wanting to learn more or wanting to share something quickly with their team or online. These might be books, blogs, articles, YouTube videos or TED Talks. There are links to any papers or internet sources that I have specifically referred to. A full list of references can be found at the end of the book.

Parting Shot

A brief summary is provided at the end of each chapter. If you take only one thing from it, make it this. I hope each parting shot will also be useful as a super-fast reminder if you want a quick recap later on.

CHAPTER ONE

LIES

You aren't being honest with yourself –
don't worry; it's entirely normal

THE REALLY BIG IDEA

There is a quote I love to use from the Harvard economist
J. K. Galbraith:

**Faced with the choice between changing one's mind
and proving that there is no need to do so, almost
everyone gets busy on the proof.**

This underpins a theme that recurs throughout this book.
The theme is quite easy to explain, but in my personal and
professional experience it's the hardest psychological concept
to get your head round which in turn makes it hard to use in
real life. Let's make it simple.

You are being lied to.

That's right. Even when amongst your carefully selected friends and when your clever mind is fully functioning and not tired/hungover/sleep deprived/stressed (delete as appropriate), someone is lying to you every day and you don't even notice.

There is a good reason that you don't notice. The person lying to you is the last person you would suspect. You've known them for ever. You'd trust them with your life.

The person lying to you is you.

Let's just pause there for a moment and allow that to sink in.

We love to think of ourselves as rational, clever, realistic and honest – and we are, for the most part – but the curiosity of the human brain means that we are also *not* rational, clever, realistic and honest.

I have tried not to use too many psychological or neurological terms in this book – mostly because they are hard to remember and aren't really the sort of phrases you want to drop into everyday conversations – but there is an exception to the rule and it's these two words: **Cognitive Dissonance**.

Let's break it down (one of my pet hates being when people use words and assume that they are in everyone's everyday vocabulary).

'Cognitive', or 'cognition', relates to your conscious intellect – the processes of thinking, remembering, understanding, imagining, reasoning or learning. If you have ever done a cognitive reasoning test to get a job, it would have been to assess how good your brain was at thinking things through. Simply put, cognitive means the process of thinking or understanding something.

'Dissonance' is when things don't match. It's often used in music to describe notes that clash discordantly. More generally it indicates a lack of harmony or agreement.

Putting the two things together – cognitive dissonance – describes a situation in which your brain is unhappy because it has received two conflicting pieces of information.

What happens next as your brain finds a way to regain harmony is fascinating. Faced with a second input that doesn't match the first, your brain quickly and conveniently changes it slightly (or even greatly) to align it with what it already knows.

Your brain may even encourage you to disregard the new data by telling you it's not important or not relevant, or that you don't have time to think about it. The problem is that by doing these things to return to equilibrium, your brain also makes the 'truth' rather murky. We believe ourselves and the evidence of our own conclusions. So, when you tell yourself that something is not important, you genuinely believe it's not important. When you tell yourself that you don't have time to think about something, you can immediately list a whole raft of more important demands on your time.

Because we can't see, feel or touch our mental or cognitive processes, it can be hard to accept how they affect us.

To make sense of this, let's take an altogether more straight-forward scenario that you could see, feel or touch. If you have ever heard a child practising piano or violin you will know how hard it is on the ears when dissonant notes are played at high volume. It's uncomfortable, annoying and exhausting to listen to. You would consider it very 'normal' to distract them with the promise of an ice-cream or any other induce-ment on hand to make them stop. No one would think you were behaving strangely. Indeed, few would bat an eyelid if you stopped them taking lessons altogether. What people *would* find strange is if you were to let the torture continue and encourage them to come closer and play louder. Imagine how stressful it would be to put up with such caterwauling for weeks on end until the noise started to resemble something tuneful – or your ears adapted to the new style of 'music'?

We can't hear our mental processes like we can an instru-ment, but a similar thing happens. When your brain believes something to be true and it receives a new piece of informa-tion that clashes with an existing belief, it doesn't like it at all. This 'dislike' is cognitive dissonance. Knowing what happens in your brain when it occurs might just change your life ...

Cognitive dissonance affects us constantly, at home and at work and from childhood upwards. Ever had a partner who everyone else could see was trouble but you thought was 'the one'? That probably didn't end well, did it?

One pretty reliable 'trick' that your brain plays on you which helps explain cognitive dissonance is called 'confirmation bias'. Your brain is wired to make you look for evidence for what you already believe to be true. When we have come to a conclusion about something or someone, our brain is continually on the lookout for more information that matches what it already thinks is right. We like to 'back-up' conclusions we have already reached.

This is related to something called the 'frequency illusion'. Have you ever bought a new car thinking it was quite an unusual make or colour and then seen hundreds of them on the road? Or you buy some cool new shoes and then everyone seems to have a similar pair? It stands to reason that there are not suddenly lots more of those particular cars or shoes in the world. The explanation is that, in order to stay sane, your brain must quickly disregard almost all of the millions of bits of information it receives every day. However, if you suddenly prompt it to think that hybrid vehicles or yellow Jimmy Choos are of interest then, guess what? Yes! There are plenty of both waiting to be noticed.

To illustrate the concept in the workplace, think about someone you consider to be a really good performer and someone else who you think is a bit flaky. You might be right. Your good performer may do only great things. Your poor performer may be a total waste of space. But be careful – your brain might also be lying to you. It might only be noticing the good things your 'good' performer does, and only noticing your flaky performer being late or on Twitter.

And when your eyes see your good performer being late – what does your brain do with the information that it gets from your eyes and needs to process? It will try the same

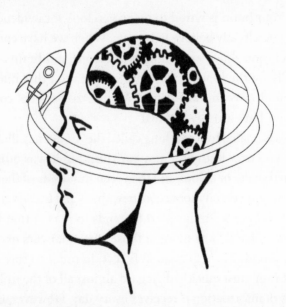

tricks as it would to stop the unmusical child's racket, to distract you from the possibility of a problem as quickly as possible.

If you could hear your brain cogs whirring around, you would probably hear something like: 'Oooh bit of cognitive dissonance there – they are late and that doesn't fit with my existing beliefs that they are "good". I'm not keen on the evidence of them being late because it goes against what I already believe to be true ... I might have to change what I think about them. Quick! Let me find some evidence it doesn't matter ... I bet there's a good reason they were late today ... I'll worry about it next time ...'

And even when next time comes your brain will find another distraction: 'Oh, they are late again ... I wonder if

I should think about that … I might do but actually I need to look at this super-important thing that has to be done right now …'

We find it easy to discover evidence for what we already believe to be true

We find it easy to discover evidence for what we already believe to be true. It is almost impossible for our brain to process evidence that something we believe to be true is not actually true after all. The reason is a very good one: being wrong takes up a lot of energy. Our brain likes patterns and order and evidence we are 'right' because that doesn't expend much cognitive energy. Our brains are actually cognitive 'misers' – wired to avoid wasting energy. In lots of ways that is a good thing. Imagine how exhausting it would be to notice every car, shoe or event that contradicts something you consider to be important or unimportant? You'd be drained half an hour after you got out of bed.

The downside is that you can't trust your brain. In an effort to conserve energy it is misleading you constantly. And the process happens so quickly and feels so natural that unless we stop to reflect, we rarely think about our thinking.

This is where I hope this book will help. By accepting that what you think or believe right now, about yourself or the people around you, might not be 'true', and might actually be the result of your brain trying to conserve energy, you can start to notice things differently.

You can start to think about your thinking. You can begin to use your cognitive processes to understand where you could improve your performance in areas you might not have noticed – even if you are already successful.

Or maybe you'll notice something that will help someone in your team to improve their performance – even if you had all but written them off.

So, perhaps our J. K. Galbraith quote is now easier to appreciate:

Faced with the choice between changing one's mind and proving that there is no need to do so, almost everyone gets busy on the proof.

I hope this founding chapter together with the rest of the book helps you to do something different. To become the exception to the rule and get less 'busy on the proof'. To divert that precious brain energy into seriously questioning whether there are some fantastic things that you could do with your brain to improve your performance and increase your happiness.

GOT IT – NOW WHAT?

Here are some of the common cognitive 'biases' or brain tricks that our brains play on us all. I very much like to call them LIES. I find that the provocative language and shock value helps people to want to overcome them.

One of the best ways to make sure that these tricks/lies don't take hold is to have some quick ways to sense-check and deliberately challenge whether they are 'real' or a trick. If not, then what you believe to be a TRUE FACT, might actually be an illusion that is holding you back from thinking about something with clarity.

Once your brain has said 'it doesn't matter', that thought will become FACT quickly

If your brain does play one of these tricks on you, sooner is better than later in terms of recognising it. Once your brain has said 'it doesn't matter' or 'I don't have time to deal with this', that thought will become FACT quickly. You will then be able to find evidence that it is TRUE that you don't have time or it doesn't matter, making it difficult to argue yourself out of that position.

Get into the habit of spotting the lies as quickly as you can. Get other people to help you. Sharing the following examples of common (and very normal) lies or biases with them can help. Give them clear and explicit permission to let you know if they hear your brain playing tricks on you. Don't dismiss their feedback if they do dare to challenge you, though. They might not do it twice ... Here are some of your brain's favourite tricks ...

 ### Brain trick 1: bandwagon effect

This is where you tell yourself that *everyone* agrees or disagrees with something so it must be right. This can happen when you talk about someone – perhaps saying you think they are a star performer and whomever you are speaking to says, 'I think you are

21

right'. Or you complain that something your boss has done is unfair and they concur. It only takes one or two people to agree with you for your brain to embed as FACT that 'Joe is a star' or that 'The new policy is unfair and possibly illegal'.

The effect of cognitive dissonance means that once you are on that bandwagon it is really hard to get off it again. Your brain is much more likely to dismiss the times when Joe is in fact not a star at all, but actually is taking advantage. Or when someone tries to point out to you that the new policy might be unpopular but it's neither unjust nor unlawful.

Here are three quick counter-measures to try:

Jump off

Deliberately jump off the bandwagon. Even just for thirty seconds of thinking time. When you find someone who agrees with you, think of a person you usually don't agree with. Ask them for a view. We do subconsciously tend to ask for opinions from people we like and who are likely to agree with us. Test out your FACT by asking someone from outside your usual circle – and really listen to what they tell you.

Pause and brainstorm the opposite

Write down the situation as if the opposite were true. If your star performer Joe was actually just talking a good game, what would you be able to see if you looked for it hard enough? If the unjust new policy was actually fair, what could it be trying to achieve? This can help your brain to notice alternative evidence. You might still want to dismiss it, but this is a little bit harder when you can see it in black and white.

Woah, Horsey!

Practise being the person who puts the brake on. Asking questions like 'How will we double check Joe isn't a poor performer in disguise?' or 'Are we sure this policy is unfair?' – One of my favourite questions in this space is 'What would we say to play devil's advocate?' My experience is that, whilst you might get some disgruntled looks to start with, people do appreciate and admire the provocative thinking and the challenge.

 ## Brain trick 2: post rationalisation

We are scarily good at telling ourselves that, in retrospect, the decisions we took are reasonable and rational. Or even when decisions are proved wrong, they were 'justified under the circumstances' or we 'had no choice' but to make them.

Our brains are well equipped (some would argue deliberately designed) to protect us from the shame of being wrong. It is really difficult to say to yourself, 'Do you know, in hindsight I could simply have done that better – no excuses.' When we are given feedback, we often find it difficult to absorb the most hurtful criticism – so we might concentrate on the parts we know are true and are less difficult to hear and just explain away the really hard bit by saying, 'They don't really know me all that well' or 'I couldn't do what they suggested for a good reason that they don't appreciate.' We can spend hours finding justification for our actions, our thoughts and our words. Frankly, this is a waste of time and energy.

Here are some tactics to challenge post rationalisation:

Welcome challenge

Let a trusted colleague or friend know that you want them to challenge you nicely when you seem to be justifying something that you did or said. Let them know that you would really welcome them saying something like, 'Is there an element of you justifying that to yourself to make you feel better about it?' Feedback can really help with this bias – but only if you listen and don't shoot the messenger.

Make failure OK

This is a really hard one, but practise telling yourself and others you trust that, whilst you know you made a mistake, it is OK because the most important thing is that you learnt X, Y or Z. It can pay to remember that we sometimes learn more from getting things wrong than we do from getting them right.

Focus forward

Practise being the person that makes it OK for other people to experience the 'shame' of having made a poor decision. Help them refocus quickly on the future rather than rewrite the facts of the past. It can make it easier to forgive yourself if you practise on other people. Try questions such as, 'If I told you it was perfectly OK to have got it wrong, but that it is not OK to berate yourself for it, what would you do now and next time?'

Brain trick 3: in-group bias

This bias tricks us into believing that people who we know well and are in our team are generally better performers than people who are in another team. Listen out for it. I bet you hear within a day something like: 'The new person isn't quite as good as Bob,' or 'The people I've interviewed from Claire's team don't seem to be as ambitious/driven/skilled/ well trained as my people.' Or, to give you an out-of-work example, 'He's OK, but our new striker is never going to be as good as [insert name of much loved goal-scorer who has moved on].' This bias is linked to our human need to belong to a tribe. Once you have found a tribe to belong to, you want to convince yourself you made the right choice – that your team is the best. Hence we look for evidence that our people are best and – hey presto! – we can find that evidence, no problem. The upside is that the better you get to know 'the other side', the more likely you are to appreciate the positives in what they do. So there is a relatively easy fix. Expand your tribe and make the boundaries of any team more flexible. Welcome outsiders and encourage your team to do the same. Remember, unless you do this, they are probably underestimating your abilities too, so it's definitely worth the effort!

So here are some ideas to help you do that:

Interview mindfully

If you interview someone from a different team, simply reminding yourself that this bias exists before you start the interview can help. Write 'In-group bias?' on your notes. It should sharpen up your listening skills and your ability to judge whether their responses to your question are really 'not as good as my team would give'.

Encourage curiosity

When you hear someone in your team being critical of another team, ask them questions that challenge their potential bias and increase the chances of effective collaboration. If your team are having a moan about the service provided from another team, challenge their perceptions by saying something like,

'Have you actually spoken to them or are you making that assumption based on their response to your email?' or, 'Go and try to get to know them a little better – it might help you to see where they are coming from and vice versa.'

Brain trick 4: status-quo bias

We love to think we embrace change and challenge. But actually, unless we instigate a change, our brain would prefer things to stay as they are. Remember the idea of your brain as a cognitive miser – it is designed to expend the minimum amount of energy necessary to get the job done. Because new things take up more energy to think about, your brain prefers the tried and tested ways of doing things. So if you find yourself coming up with a great idea but can't seem to find the impetus to get started, or tell yourself 'I'll start tomorrow' or 'It's not broken, so why fix it?' your brain could well be playing a trick on you. Something might not be broken, but it could work much better if you stopped listening to your own excuses.

Remember...
your brain is a
cognitive miser

Try these ideas to get your brain to be less miserly about new concepts:

Just take 10

If you find yourself feeling less than enthusiastic about a new idea, promise yourself that you will try it for ten minutes straight away, before your brain gets a head of steam and convinces you not to bother. During that ten minutes, don't allow yourself to look for reasons that it won't work – stay positive that it could. At the end of the ten minutes do a quick brainstorm and write down three positive reasons for its implementation. Chances are that, having tried it for ten minutes, your brain has already invested some energy and won't want that to go to waste. Many of my clients have fed back that this 'ten minute' trick works really well. I use it when I am in a coaching session sometimes and I have seen it achieve great results for my clients.

People generally have an hour or ninety minutes in their diary booked for our session. When I hear them making excuses about why something won't work, I ask them to take a break to try out the 'new thing' for ten minutes. They can't use the excuse 'I don't have time' because I have just provided it! I explain that this will enable us to explore together in the immediate aftermath of that ten-minute consideration whether they think at all differently about doing something different. In my experience, clients find they are much more positive by the end of just ten minutes.

Quick brainstorm

If you find yourself or anyone else saying 'It's not broken ...' when you are faced with a new idea for adapting or changing something that is not brilliant, take a moment to do a quick brainstorm. On paper works best. Write down all the potential opportunities that could arise from it being 'great' not just 'OK'. As well as the obvious things, ask yourself 'What is the very best thing that could happen?' and 'What left-field, entirely different things could this lead to if it worked like a charm?' or 'What would happen in my wildest dreams?' Actively encourage your imagination to run riot for a minute or two. There is some evidence that this releases dopamine and serotonin – two hormones that can make you feel happier and more motivated. These natural chemicals can sometimes help get you started.

The most certain way to prevent your brain creating a fabulous opportunity from a new idea is to not give it a chance.

 ## Brain trick 5: self-serving bias

Human beings are really good at thinking that the skills and qualities that have helped us to be good parents or successful in our jobs will help other people too. Equally, whilst we might appreciate that people are different, we can easily convince ourselves that a skill or quality that we *don't* have is actually not that important after all. It's easy to see why. If someone asks us how we achieved something, we tell them what we did or didn't do. It becomes natural therefore to equate that 'success' directly with those actions. We have 'evidence' that what we did or didn't do 'worked', and our brain wants to repeat that pattern. We miss that something else could have worked just as well.

I describe this science most often when I am asked to help a client to develop their leadership criteria, or their 'people' specifications for use in recruitment. The problem is that if you ask the people currently in the business to give you their 'people-spec', then as human beings they will advocate the inclusion of those qualities or skills that they believe have contributed to their own success. Equally, they will often argue that skills or qualities they don't possess are of less importance or relevance – and why wouldn't they, since they have very little personal 'evidence' that those 'other' things matter?

We can create evidence aplenty that there is a workaround for any deficiencies – because we have worked around them!

With that in mind, here are some things to think about:

Interview mindfully (again)

We can tend to recruit in our own image. If you are interviewing someone, beware of this bias. You might think that one candidate who gives you all the right answers is perfect for the job. However, the 'right' answer could simply be the one you would have given. Someone who gives you an entirely different answer from the one you were expecting (or even an answer that you think is 'wrong') might be a great candidate. Perhaps they have a different set of skills and strengths that would be equally or even more useful in your team or company? Do they have strengths and skills that complement your own rather than mirror them?

Work with 'That won't work'

If you find yourself saying, 'That won't work,' consider whether what you *actually* mean is, 'I don't have personal evidence that will work.' We can sometimes be quick to dismiss an idea simply because our brain doesn't want to expend the energy on thinking about something new. Remember, your brain is a miser.

Catch it and call it out

Be wary of sentences that begin 'You should try this – it works for me,' or 'Don't bother – I tried it and it didn't work.' Whether this is something you hear yourself saying or something you are on the receiving end of, don't be surprised if the well-intentioned advice isn't acted upon. With just a little knowledge of self-serving bias, we can perhaps see that, whilst offering advice based on what worked for you can be helpful, it can also easily fall on deaf ears. 'Don't try and operate that machine with wet hands' might be a life-saver. When it comes to a situation where there are infinite variables such as how to lead a team, the polar opposite of what you felt worked really well for you personally might play to the strengths of someone else. There's more about this bias in Chapter 6 when we talk about diversity and in Chapter 10 when we discuss coaching.

  ## Brain trick 6: negativity bias

I find this one particularly fascinating and I only learnt about it around five years ago. Basically, we are wired to think that people who are critical and negative have more gravitas, and even to assume they are smarter than someone who is enthusiastic and smiley. This can mean that we are likely to take feedback from Mr Grumpy to heart but will pay less attention to a positive comment from Little Miss Sunshine.

I wish I had known about it when I first used to go to executive meetings to present ideas. I noticed a pattern that I didn't understand at the time. I would find that members of a senior team would be quite positive or even enthusiastic in their support for an idea when I spoke to them privately – 'Sounds like a great idea – let's get you to the Exec to present it,' or, 'That sounds challenging, but I'm sure we could find a way.' However, in the more formal meetings when they were joined by senior colleagues, those positive feelings seemed subdued or muted and were replaced by more reluctance than I was expecting from those previously enthusiastic people – and it seemed to be catching. Comments – by someone who had been enthusiastic about an idea one to one – like 'I'm still not a hundred per cent convinced this can work' took me by surprise. I also noticed that it influenced the room to ask for more information and a delay in introducing an idea. Clearly, a formal meeting will always be more structured and considered than an informal chat in someone's office, but often the atmosphere seemed subtly more critical and negative.

With the benefit of knowing the brain tricks about bandwagons, the status quo and negativity, I now reflect that it is not at all surprising that any private enthusiasm or excitement for a new idea has a very hard time being displayed in a 'serious' environment. Given that we associate negativity and criticism with gravitas and intellect, it is no surprise that we subconsciously 'upweight' those qualities when we are in the boardroom. Imagine a scenario where one or two of the most senior people in the room are critical of an idea. Even if those two individuals are simply feeling a human bias towards the status quo and the idea is a brilliant one, how difficult do you think our brains would find it to enthusiastically argue against their clever sounding caution if we were sat at a table in a less senior role? Our brains tell us we won't look clever, and that it is much safer to align ourselves with the status quo and the top gun in the room.

Knowing about negativity bias means that I don't respond to negativity in formal meetings in the way I once did. I used to take it quite personally – I can remember feeling quite 'betrayed' and being made angry and emotional by some of the responses of previously supportive colleagues – but being able to attribute it to negativity bias helps me to remain calm and respond in a more balanced way.

I have worked with some executives who are very gifted at getting their colleagues to be their more positive selves during a meeting. They are sensitive to an atmosphere of unhelpful negativity and caution and sometimes will be 'provocatively positive' or look to make decisions in less formal settings than a boardroom.

No one would suggest that it makes commercial or practical sense to run a business, a school, a hospital or even a family by enthusiastically implementing every idea that comes along without sitting down and thinking about its merits. However, it can be helpful to consciously remind ourselves that, when we are in a group where our status matters and a new idea is introduced, our brains feel safer with what is familiar and will bias us towards the negative. Otherwise something left-field but brilliant could get sidelined because our very human brains come up with a million reasons not to do it.

Here are some thoughts to help your brain accept that it can be enthusiastic AND clever:

Influence-matrix activity

As human beings we are generally motivated to seek approval and copy the behaviour of influential people and to distance ourselves from or disagree with those who have lower influence. It's called the 'influence matrix'. Try this experiment when you are next the most senior or most influential person in a meeting, see what happens when you are positive about an idea first and, conversely, what happens when you are immediately critical. Do both in the same meeting and observe the reactions around you carefully. Repeat over a series of meetings. Does negativity bias seem to affect some of your team more than others? You can easily overlook the fact that you are surrounded by 'yes' men and women. Noticing it could help you survive (ask Enron) and enhance your ability to make the most of the opportunities available to you.

Don't slow down

Ask yourself which decisions are best made 'away from the table' and which need proper and formal consideration. In my experience, businesses can get tied up in negative bureaucracy and endless meeting cycles that slows things down unduly. Part of the reason could be due to the natural negativity trick that our brains play on us all.

Be positive on purpose

Force yourself and other people around you to think of a positive or a potential solution to each negative they raise. When people say 'It simply won't work', try asking 'Let's challenge our thinking for a moment. If our business survival depended on making it work, what could we do?'

Exceptional executives

If you are part of an executive committee or a senior formal meeting, my favourite short research paper to recommend is from the *Harvard Business Review* and is entitled 'What Makes Great Boards Great'. Jeffrey Sonnerfeld writes: 'What distinguishes exemplary boards is that they are robust, effective social systems with a virtuous circle of respect, trust and candour.' There is more on why trust AND challenge together are important in Chapter 9, for executives and indeed anyone else. For now, reading this short paper could help you to have candour, without undue negativity.

 ## Brain trick 7: current-moment bias

I bet your tricky brain has tried this one on you at least a half dozen times today already! Your brain regards 'right now' as very 'precious'. Don't forget, your brain is a miser. The miserly trick it plays here is to protect the 'current moment' – encouraging you only to do things right now that are easy, you have done before and like doing. Remember, this is not because the easy things are necessarily the best way to use your precious time (although your brain, in trying to conserve metabolic resources, might make you think they are). Your brain will come up with all sorts of sentences to make you feel it is perfectly rational that more difficult conversations, and other things that will take up a lot of cognitive 'energy' are not worth doing. Your brain will try all sorts – ever thought … 'I'll do a better job on that in the morning, when I'm fresh,' or, 'I'll focus on that next, when I've got more time,' or, 'That difficult conversation with Tom will be more productive if I have spoken to Joe first and reviewed his objectives properly.'

Be honest. How many of those things that you neatly convince yourself to do 'tomorrow' actually happen the very next day? Or is it more likely that they then get placed on the list for the day after that? Or the day after that?

This is because, once 'tomorrow' or 'next week' becomes 'today' our current-moment bias kicks in again. If you are not careful, you end up with a to-do list as long as your arm and spend so long curating it and rewriting it that you actually reduce the amount of time available to get things done.

Here are some possible remedies:

The 4 Ds

It's a fabulous return trick! Try it right now. Look at your to-do list or try it when a request comes into your inbox. Do one of the 4 Ds immediately – either:

1. **DO** it now. Yep. Right Now. You will then have only thought about it once and read the email one time. This can save you hours. Otherwise you have to remember to remember it (or find and re-read the email), which takes up valuable thinking time you can invest elsewhere.

2. **DIARISE** it. Don't put an action on a to-do list. Put an appointment in your diary to do it. This helps you to schedule time really well – you can plan your important thinking tasks for when you know you have time to do them, or for a time of day when

you have noticed those types of tasks take you less time to do. Diarising it means that you are also appreciating you can't do something else at the same time ... More of that in Chapter 7. (Spoiler: Multitasking is almost impossible unless the quality of what you are doing doesn't matter – then it's possible – but it actually doesn't save you very much time).

3. **DELEGATE** it. Do it straight away. Give the task to someone whose strengths it plays to most closely and who will do it without you having to chase them. Be clear on what you want the person to do. Get into the habit of asking once and ensuring there are clear consequences when you have to ask twice. (By 'consequences', I don't mean being fired. An uncomfortable conversation using some of the 'Top Right Questions' in this book will mean you keep your people *and* get them to be more effective.)

4. **DITCH** it. Yes you read that one right. Be realistic. If something is not important enough to you, and you will probably put it off until it is too late, then ditch it now, before you have invested any more energy on it. If you aren't going to remember to send back the feedback request and don't really have much to say then just delete or bin the request now. Even if you do send a quick note

of apology to explain why you won't be doing something, you will spend far less time on it than you will if you half-carry it around in your head or keep writing it down on a new to-do list when you know in your heart of hearts you aren't going to do it.

Just take 10 (again)

Try a variation tip we've met before. When you find yourself saying 'I'll do that tomorrow/next week/ when I'm ready', deliberately stop yourself putting it off and instead do it for just ten minutes. It can be so hard to resist postponing a difficult conversation or a boring job. But I promise you, I've tested this ricochet trick with hundreds of clients and friends over the years. More than 99 per cent report back that they are pleased they did it and it wasn't so bad after all once they picked the phone up or got started.

Brain trick 8: false-consensus bias

You might have noticed this bias if you have had friends round to dinner recently and suddenly realised they don't share your views on something in the news and were really surprised. Apparently we are much more likely to think people will agree with us if we like them and can be surprised when they disagree or say they won't back our idea. The converse is true. We are surprised when people we don't like or don't know well wholeheartedly agree and support us.

When we are making decisions and trying to win people over, if we are not careful we don't listen to the warning signs that someone we like is trying to break to us gently that they don't agree ... We can mistakenly take a 'Mmm – let me think about it' as a firm yes.

Combine this bias with the in-group bias we talked about above and your brain can think of some nifty excuses not to look outside your team for feedback 'because it won't help'. We might put off from asking for feedback from people we often cross swords with when actually they might fundamentally agree with us. Even if they have a couple of challenging observations, the bonus is that asking people you don't know well or have previously argued with about something is an opportunity to build the relationship too.

Here's some quick ways to test this out:

Go walkabout
If you have an idea or need some feedback about something right now, walk away from your desk and go for a wander. Find someone you don't know very well or haven't always seen eye to eye with and

request a minute of their time to ask for their feedback. It could be the start of a beautifully productive friendship.

Make it safe for people to tell you what they really think

Listen for what people don't say
Be careful about assuming that you know what people think because you do or don't like them. It's natural, but dangerous. When you next get a less than extremely enthusiastic reply from someone you know and love, make it safe for them to tell you what they really think. Questions that reassure them, such as 'I'm sensing you don't totally agree – that's OK – I'd love to know what you really think', can help them as well as you to navigate a potential area of disagreement.

TOP RIGHT QUESTIONS

For you

➤ What have I just told myself that might not actually be true?

➤ If I were to convince myself the opposite were true, what evidence would I look for?

➤ If I find some contradictory evidence, what will I need to do in order to pay attention to it?

➤ Who could challenge me to know this is true and not just my brain playing tricks on me?

For others

➤ What emotion might your brain be trying to avoid?

➤ If you could think of failure as a bruise and not a tattoo what would you do?

LEARN MORE AND SHARE

Really great read

A Mind of Its Own by Cordelia Fine

Cordelia Fine is a psychologist with a degree from Oxford, Masters from Cambridge, PhD from UCL and is a professor at the University of Melbourne.

Blogs

A one page blog on the dreaded 'to do' list and getting them done:

https://changeyourmindfast.com/2015/03/26/just-one-thing/

A quick Christmas blog on coping with multiple demands on your time, that resonates any time of the year:

https://toprightthinking.com/2017/12/14/a-christmas-miracle/

Article

Jeffrey Sonnenfeld's *Harvard Business Review* article explains why great boards are as much about highly functioning social systems as bringing together experience:

https://hbr.org/2002/09/what-makes-great-boards-great

PARTING SHOT

It can be exhausting to start thinking about your thinking. It can also be disconcerting to have held a belief for twenty-five years and then to realise that what you have been telling yourself is crucial to your success might have been a lie that has held you back in some way. But the realisation that your brain is playing tricks on you can be revelatory. Some of the lighter-hearted 'lies' my brain told me over the past twenty years include 'You'll never be able to play an instrument – you can't read music,' and 'I'd have loved to have learnt to surf when I was younger – it's too late now.' I turned forty thinking those ships had sailed.

Now I know about brain lies, I practise fun ways of proving I can get past them. As a result, I was in the North Sea last November on a surfboard to see off a particularly spectacular hangover. I play the guitar and sing along whenever I get the chance – I will leave you to imagine what my teenage children make of that … But this gives me 'evidence' I can use as motivation to tackle the more pedestrian work-day lies too.

Who says you can't teach an old dog new tricks? Not I. Not any more. The old dog just needs to disregard its brain when it spouts all sorts of lies about the new tricks being unnecessary new-fangled nonsense and therefore not worth the effort of learning.

Let's tackle your 'old dog'. On to Chapter 2.

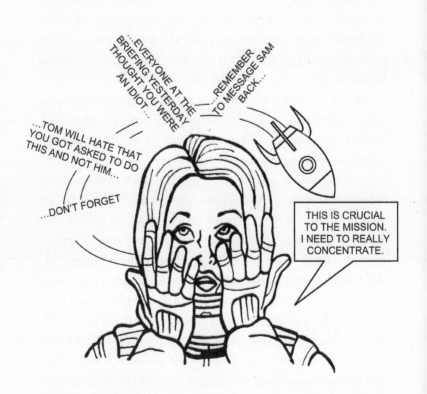

CHAPTER TWO

DON'T WORK HARDER

Think better

THE REALLY BIG IDEA

Most people know that the brain has different sections, and those sections have different purposes. We might not know what the parts are called or exactly what they do, but most of us know that some areas of the brain deal with conscious thoughts, some deal with emotions and some deal with things we do unconsciously like breathing or heat control.

Without getting too technical, one of the things I often end up talking about with my clients is how relatively small the 'clever' bit of your brain is. By the 'clever' bit I mean the part that deals with conscious thought, or 'cognitive function' to use a technical term. We met this bit of the brain in Chapter 1 when we talked about 'cognitive dissonance'. Our cognitive functions are the things we do consciously – learning new things, memorising and recalling, making sense or under-standing, deciding between alternatives, imagining what could happen and making predictions. Last but by no means least (because it is exhausting!) it also controls inhibition. Trying to avoid those things that we know aren't useful or helpful, but that we can't seem to resist doing.

The technical term for this 'clever' part of your brain is the prefrontal cortex. It surprises lots of people I talk to, given everything that it is responsible for, that this hard-working bit of tissue makes up less than 5 per cent of the volume of your brain.

Clients often tell me that they are feeling overwhelmed. They describe their impossible workload and how they are far too busy to cope. They might tell me that their brain feels 'too full' and they can't think.

One of the first things I do is reassure them that this is quite normal, given how small the part of the brain is they are using to complete most of their work.

Take a moment to think about the things you are going to do today. It's extremely likely that you will require this small part of your brain for all of them. You will move between learning something, memorising something, remembering something, deciding upon something, making sense of some-thing, imagining what could happen to someone or some-thing. You might even use it to resist a biscuit.

Not only is the area of your brain that processes all these

things really small – in our human evolution, it was also the last bit to develop. When I describe it to a burnt-out client, I get them to imagine a simplified version of our human history so that they can more easily visualise the impact of those thousands of years.

The human brain we have now took thousands of years to evolve. It was 95 per cent finished and then, right at the last minute, we discovered a need to be intellectual and to think. There was just a tiny space left at the front where this 'clever' bit could be squeezed in. There's no real room for it to grow and develop, which is why it can only do one thing at a time. It might evolve in the future, but for now the prefrontal cortex is a bit like an old-style light bulb that requires a lot of energy. It is also last in the brain-queue for any energy we have spare – we can't decide to stop breathing or pause our heartbeat to give us more thinking space.

Our whole body requires metabolic energy to operate. In simple terms this 'fuel' derives from blood, oxygen and glucose. Those resources are limited – we don't carry an infinite supply – hence we need to replenish our stocks by resting.

We understand the metabolic impact of energy reserves and their use about other parts of our body that we can see, feel and touch – for example we don't find it strange that our legs can't sprint hard for more than about ten seconds without needing a rest. We would think bizarre the suggestion that anyone could run at this pace for hours – we would simply understand it was impossible.

When we think about our brain in this way, it starts to make sense that we struggle sometimes to juggle all the things we have to do in a day. We are trying to do all those different tasks using one tiny part of our brain that is shoehorned in, not yet efficient enough to do two things at once and that takes far more blood, oxygen and glucose to run than other parts of the brain. The clever bit is doing the best job it can; however, with limited room and finite resources, it is simply not as efficient as we would want it to be, and we can't force it to be more efficient by working harder. Our biology means that is impossible.

It doesn't matter how smart you think you are – ask this part of your brain to do two things at once and it can't do both with the accuracy it could achieve by doing one at a time. You will know this for yourself – have you ever tried to remember a song whilst another song is playing in the background? Or – try this now – perhaps recite the alphabet backwards and then see if you can do it whilst typing out an email. Or next time you are using a hammer to put a nail in a wall to hang a picture – or maybe not . .

This is not new science. One of the first experiments in this field was conducted in the 1890s by a scientist called J. C. Welsh. She measured the strength of people's grip using a dynamometer (you can buy these online as we speak – apparently gripping one daily is a scientifically proven way to reduce your blood pressure). She asked people to grip as hard as they could and measured what happened to the strength of the grip if she gave people a mental task to do at the same time. She showed that the strength of the grip reduced dramatically when people were thinking about something else – commonly by as much as 50 per cent.

My favourite piece of research to provoke thinking about distraction, multitasking and the modern trend of always being 'switched on' comes courtesy of a controversial study by Glenn Wilson, a psychologist from King's College, London. He found that constant access to email and texts as a way of 'multitasking' reduces the IQ of men by fifteen points and women by five points. This might be part of the reason why there is a myth that women can multitask 'better' than men … But the truth is no one can multitask without the quality of the result suffering and no one can keep making good decisions without a break.

The BBC programme *Twinstitute* carried out an experiment in a similar vein in January 2019. The premise of the show, which is presented by two medical doctors who are also twin brothers, is to take pairs of identical twins and scientifically test two different ways of improving health by assessing two different ways of doing something head to head.

One of their experiments involved splitting the twins into two groups and getting them to do an IQ test. One group did the test with their smartphone on the table. The second group had their phone taken away from them at the door to the examination room. It was found that the twin with the phone on the table performed on average ten points worse than the twin who couldn't see their phone.

It was not the distraction of an actual call or text that was responsible for the lower IQ results – no one actually used their phone during the test – but the sheer presence of the phone. Being reminded by association that something might have happened on social media they'd like to know about, for example. Our brains are less efficient (so use more energy and need to think about something for longer) when we 'switch' from one task to another and try to do two things in parallel rather than completing one and then moving on to the other.

Remember, the small 'clever' part of our brain is not just responsible for answering an exam question and deciding if the answer is A, B or C; it is also responsible for imagining who might call or remembering that you need to order something online. When it is doing one of those activities, it can't do another one efficiently. It is likely that the twin with the phone on the desk was inadvertently switching between tasks – between doing the IQ test and wondering briefly what was the latest news headline. The results of this experiment showed just how easily we get distracted – and how simple it can be to 'allow' our brains to be less efficient.

There might be a few differences on the edges – some people might be able to focus for longer than others, but those differences are marginal. We all have the same biology. We all have basically the same brain, of which just 5 per cent is given over to conscious 'clever' thought. To imagine that some people have found a way around this limitation is like being told that someone can run at Usain Bolt's pace for six hours. You simply wouldn't believe them.

Another more recent experiment showed the potentially dramatic impact on our decision making when we refuel our tired brains. In a paper published in the National Academy of Science USA in 2011, Kurt Danziger, who studied at Oxford and Melbourne, did a study to look at the impact of rest and refuelling on the decisions made by a parole board. His experiment found that the last prisoner to be seen before the mid-morning break had an almost 0 per cent chance of obtaining parole. Immediately after the break, during which the judges ate a sandwich and piece of fruit, their chances of parole increased to around 65 per cent.

As ever, science is evolving, and there have been subsequent studies that have questioned whether all of this 65 per cent differential can be attributed to a rest and a sandwich. For our purposes, we don't need to get involved in the academic debate. Safe to say there is a significant connection proved by this study and many similar ones between our decision-making capabilities and whether we have taken a break to replenish our glucose levels. We can be confident that once we have made one decision, we have significantly less resources to make the next decision unless we stop to refuel. You can't just keep the quality of your thinking going by telling it to power on. You have to stop and refuel, or you will simply be unable to do your best thinking. Just as you would have to stop after one sprint and take a breather before you were able to do another.

If we accept what the science has proven – that you can't do two things at once without diminished quality, that you have to refuel to do your best thinking, that the tiny 'clever' bit of your brain is energy hungry, not very efficient or far too easily distracted for our own good – what can we do? Does it mean that

You can't do two things at once without diminished quality

you can't actually have a busy job, loads of family commitments and a social life? Can you really not have it all?

I don't think it does mean that. I think you can 'have it all'. You just have to find ways to get your best game-brain on.

Before you tell yourself that your workload is impossible and that you will never be able to get everything done today, or that you can never be both a good parent *and* a high flyer, or you don't have time to get fit … Pause. Stop. Think. The science doesn't say that. It does, however, tell us that to win the Game of Life, you will benefit from living it with some new and more productive 'brain-tricks' up your sleeve. I hope I might already have influenced you to use the 4 Ds as a more effective way of organising your tasks (**see p. 38**). When your brain pitches you a curve ball, some of these other tricks will enable you to bat it back.

GOT IT – NOW WHAT?

Minimise distractions

It sounds obvious and simple, but most of us don't actively look to avoid distractions as much as we should. In my experience this happens less often when we know we have a big job to do – most of us will at some stage have locked ourselves away to work on something important in peace.

It pays to think about your smaller daily challenges, if you have accepted that your brain can't multitask, that it takes energy to switch from one thing to another and that your brain loves a distraction, then hopefully you will accept that some of the things that 'help' your brain to get distracted every day are worth thinking about too.

Some of the distractions are technological and initially seem helpful – until you know the science. If you have an email pop-up, for example, there is no doubt that it will help you not to miss an important notification, but every time a notification pops up we have to accept that we expend additional brain energy as we glance at it before focusing back on the job at hand. Turning this function off – even temporarily, will mean that you save brain energy and time on those days you are feeling really pushed. We can then choose to reinvest that time and energy into something else.

Putting your phone away or hiding it behind your laptop is another quick tip to make sure you don't suffer from that five (or fifteen!) point IQ drop.

Simplify

If something is quite complicated to understand or explain, try to simplify it first – so that you and anyone to whom you are trying to explain it can get their head moving in the right direction first. Asking yourself or others to imagine things that are innovative takes up a lot of energy. We find it much easier to imagine something that is *similar* to something we are already familiar with.

Powerful Pitching for Film & TV Screenwriters, a book written to help screenwriters and other cinema and TV professionals to pitch their ideas, is a great place to start to learn the art of simplification. In the book Charles Harris tells this story:

Two screenwriters walk into a Hollywood producer's office and say three words – 'Jaws in Space'. Those three words won them the contract for the film *Alien*.

If you are confused about a task that someone has given you, use the simplify principle to clarify what they mean rather than spending hours and wasting lots of that precious brain energy trying to make sense of it. You can get to a surprising level of understanding much more quickly if you ask things at the outset such as, 'Would you be able to draw what the finished result looks like?' or, 'If you were to encapsulate what a really good job looks like in two sentences, what would they be?'

Use it to clarify what you want to get done, too. Look at your diary. Write down two sentences that describe what your priorities are today. What are the one or two key conversations or activities that will help you get what you want? Prioritise and do those first – before you get distracted or de-energised by something else.

These simplification activities take seconds, but they can really help you to focus on what is important. Try setting an hourly alarm or just check in with yourself at points during the day. Are you doing an activity that will achieve the goal you set and help you to feel how you want to feel? If not, and you have been distracted, don't worry – that is quite usual – but use the pause to get back on track. Writing your simplified goals for the day makes it easier to dismiss emails, conversations tasks or interruptions that will take up brain space but won't help you to get what you want or make you feel how you want to feel.

Think: first things first

Many people have heard of 'first things first' as a phrase from Stephen Covey's *The 7 Habits of Highly Effective People*. That's because it's a great tip that works.

Remember that your brain only has limited energy before it will need a rest. Therefore, it makes sense to do the important things first. If you don't feel you are at your best early in the day then ensure that you schedule the important things when your brain is at its best.

Many people I work with start the day by clearing their email inbox and then wonder why they feel stressed and tired. Email is undoubtedly a fantastic tool, but nearly all my clients say they receive an unhelpful amount of them.

The bottom line is that if you use your brain to clear email first then you will have used up some of your best energy of the day on other people's priorities rather than your own. This observation/tip was given to me by a hugely talented and very smart lawyer Bronagh Kennedy, now Group Company Secretary and General Counsel for Severn Trent Water, who combined having young children and an executive role. She was very open with me about how she balanced her home life whilst succeeding at the very top of a tough corporate organisation and I've never forgotten her wisdom and advice. I use this tip myself every day and pass it onto a client at least weekly.

The other problem with email is it doesn't play to your brain's strengths. To be at its best, your brain wants to finish one thing before it starts another. Email can make that feel almost impossible. If you open your inbox first and you have a hundred messages there, the first thing you are telling your brain is that there are a hundred things to deal with before you can start on your priority. In overwhelming your brain with a huge list of activities right at the start of the day, it is likely your brain will start to lie to you immediately: 'Oh, I've had too much come into my inbox, I'm too busy to start my priority today. I'll clear these today and get started tomorrow.'

There are many tools you can use to sift and sort your email, but it doesn't change the baseline scientific facts. Once our brain has worked on something, it is less efficient at the next task unless it is given time to rest and fuel to recharge. It means that once you have started to sift and sort emails, even if you only deal with the important ones, you will have a lot less brain power for whatever task you intended to prioritise.

The most simple thing I do, and something I recommend to clients, is to start the day writing down their single most important priority. I then suggest they actively do something about their priority *before* opening up email. This can be ten minutes of uninterrupted focus on the priority to think it through or 'doing' something in the more traditional sense – like chunking it down into simple steps or mapping it out. People promise me it works.

Another thing I suggest is at mid-morning, lunchtime and mid-afternoon they pause for three minutes (some set an alarm on their phones). I ask clients to use that time to think about how much time and energy they have put into their priority for the day.

This gives them three further opportunities to put first things first, not just one at the start of the day; three chances to make a correction if their brains have allowed them to prioritise something else.

Many of my clients have reported that pausing like that usually helps them realise that they have become side-tracked or distracted. They find themselves super-busy on a task-treadmill – often at the expense of the one thing they wanted to get done – and feeling nowhere near how they wanted to feel about their day.

Without a pause, their brains help them to avoid their priorities by telling them some of the brain's lies we met in Chapter 1, such as, 'I'll just finish this first,' or, 'I'll start that tomorrow when I'm fresher,' or, 'This workload is ridiculous – everyone says so.'

With a quick pause we can challenge such lies and consider whether we are working on our priorities and things we can control. The pause reminds us to take a break to refuel our brains and make a conscious decision about what to do next. Without the pause we will be busy, but we might well be directing energy to things that weren't first on our list – or even second, third or fourth. We can easily – unless we consciously stop and think – be working on other people's priorities, telling ourselves we don't have a choice and feeling resentful, stressed and overwhelmed.

It might seem counter-intuitive to stop when you are so busy, but it is only by stopping that you can refuel and refocus so that you put first things first and take control of your thinking power.

I'm not perfect. I readily acknowledge to clients that I am the queen of distractions. I love it when they call me to ask,

'Are you busy – can I ask you a quick question?' However, because I know I might not focus on my priority once the day gets going, I will always try to make up for it by giving that priority at least half an hour before I open up my email, or take my first call.

To give you a real (and potentially unwelcome) picture, the words you are reading right now are being typed in bed at 7 a.m. with a cup of tea made from my bedside Teasmade and the breakfast sandwich I put in foil last night. I do this so that I can fit in half an hour of writing before I get up to sort the kids out for school, empty the dishwasher, walk the dogs and get ready to go and train or coach someone exciting. After eight years of false starts, I realised that if I was waiting for 'some spare time' to write, or that I would 'do it when I've finished this', a book was never going to happen.

Remove your hecklers

David Rock uses an image in his book *The Brain at Work* of the prefrontal cortex as a very small stage with space for just one performer. I build on this idea to explain to clients what happens from a neuroscience perspective when we don't deal with issues or tasks straight away.

Imagine that you are a comedian on this small stage. You are telling a joke and partway through someone shouts from the audience. You can see how this would be distracting and how you would need to either consciously refocus in order to ignore the heckler, divert from your original joke with a witty put-down, or ask security to remove them. Whichever way it goes, the original joke is disturbed and the effort of refocusing to think of a retort uses brain energy that you would not have needed to expend if they had kept their mouths shut.

Things we haven't done or things we have started and haven't finished act like hecklers when we are trying to concentrate. The fact that you need to remember to book a doctor's appointment or schedule a meeting with someone is likely to shout 'Don't forget about me!' partway through another task you're concentrating on.

Imagine how distracting you would find it as a comedian, and how much brain energy it would take, if there were five hecklers in the audience. It would be exhausting. Your joke would probably never get finished. Yet most of us, every day, have way more than 5 things to remember to do.

My tip if you feel overwhelmed or heckled by tasks on your to-do list is to remember the comedian-on-stage imagery to help you notice a 'heckler'. Try to spot an example of it today or tomorrow, whilst the image is fresh in your mind.

When you realise you have become distracted, pause and ask yourself 'What is the best use of my limited energy?' Do you think you will genuinely be able to refocus and put the distracting heckler out of your mind? Or would it be more energy efficient to use one of the 4 D's from Chapter 1 (Do it now, Diarise it, Delegate it or Ditch it) to deal with the distracting heckler quickly and remove it from the audience? I sometimes add in an extra D that's actually a P – Post it. When clients are getting distracted by something, I suggest they put it on a Post-it note and stick in on the wall. The action of physically doing something with the idea or the distraction seems to help them to put it to one side, both literally and neurologically speaking.

Sometimes the thoughts that keep popping into our heads to distract us are things are we are putting off (usually courtesy of some of the lies we met in Chapter 1). Perhaps the heckler is reminding you about an uncomfortable conversation you have been putting off? Or that you still need to do that boring job you hate?

Remember that every time one of these heckling distractions happens, you are using up a little bit of brain power in order to put it to one side or to refocus. So, if that same heckler pops up more than once, you might waste more time

and brain energy on refocusing than you would on just dealing with it now. You can create extra time and energy for yourself by dealing with your distractions decisively the first time they heckle you. If it's Done, Diarised, Delegated, Ditched or Posted on the wall it is a lot less likely to interrupt you.

Should you Do it, Diarise it, Delegate it, Ditch it or Post It?

You may have come across tips before, perhaps if you have ever done a time-management course about only touching a piece of paper or reading an email once – i.e. dealing with things straight away rather than putting them in a 'to be dealt with later' pile. I like to think of this habit as stopping the heckler at the door. Getting into the good habit of using one of the 4 Ds on an email when it first arrives can stop it from turning into a heckler in the first place. Don't leave it there to read again later.

In summary, the trick is to notice hecklers, pause to deal with them and, if at all possible, keep them from even getting through the door. Notice when you are being distracted. Pause to use the 4 Ds (or 1 P) to deal with the distraction. Try to avoid the distraction by dealing with things quickly and decisively rather than letting your current-moment bias allow you to put it off for later.

Chunk things up

Your brain remembers and processes things better if the information or ideas are presented in chunks. For an easy way to prove this to yourself, say your mobile phone number out loud. Chances are you will separate out the 07XXX bit and then chunk the last six digits into pairs or groups of three.

You can use this same trick to plan your work better and therefore better harness your brainpower.

If you have a big job to get done and start to think 'I don't know where to start …' don't just dive in. Your brain might find any sort of momentum difficult to sustain. Or you may find that the whole thing feels too intimidating to tackle and lie to yourself to feel OK about putting it off until tomorrow. Instead, try to divide the job into three or four chunks. Writing down those chunks seems to help too – strangely all the better written big – on a flipchart or white board.

Zoom out before you zoom in

Your brain is not only easily distracted, but also very good at going down a rabbit hole and getting stuck – if you let it. We can be prone to overthinking and going into too much detail on the first part of a task or zooming in on a problem we find whilst doing a task and giving it too much attention. If you go down those rabbit holes, you can find that you have not left enough time to complete the overall task properly. This can particularly be the case if there is a part of a task that we enjoy. Our brain is likely to help us feel this is the most 'important' part and that we are right to be spending time on it. For example, if you like problem solving and you find a problem to solve, you can spend hours on it before realising that, in the wider scheme of things, it is actually not that important a problem.

When you have done the 'chunking' exercise above, look at how much time you have to complete the task. It can help to give yourself a rough deadline to complete each chunk.

If you find yourself stuck on a problem, ask yourself how much time you realistically have to fix it. If you have all the time in the world, great. This means that you can really get into the detail and come up with your very best solution. But let's say you have five minutes to proofread a report before you send it to your boss or to a client. If you find that your second paragraph doesn't make sense you could easily spend that precious five minutes working on it – only to find it doesn't leave you the time to proofread the rest, which might also contain errors. Just pause before you zoom in to fix paragraph two. Zoom out first.

> If you don't read the rest, how will you know that the issue in paragraph two is the most crucial thing to fix?

> If you quickly proofread the rest, how long would that leave you to rework paragraph two?

> Is paragraph two crucial? If not, could you lose it altogether and use the five minutes to proofread the rest?

Just a few seconds spent zooming out can mean that the small, clever part of your brain is focused on what it really needs to – particularly when you are short on time and you start to panic.

Use your full brain

There is an exception to the rule on multitasking. If you practise something long and hard enough, you can 'move' that skill from the prefrontal cortex to a different part of your brain called the limbic system. An easy way to explain how this works is to think about learning to drive. At your first driving lesson, the 'mirror, signal, manoeuvre' instruction would have involved the small, clever bit of your brain because you would need to have consciously thought about it and you were trying to memorise it. However, after a few years you become very used to driving and can happily talk, sing or listen to the radio as you drive along and never stop to think 'mirror, signal, manoeuvre'. That is because driving is not something you 'think' about any more – the responsibility for the task has been shifted into the limbic system which deals with automated tasks. This releases the small, clever bit of your brain to do other things like listen to an audiobook whilst driving.

You can use the same techniques to reduce the load on your brain at work. For example, one of the things that I have trained myself to do is touch type. I can now type out virtually word for word a conversation I am having and still focus on that conversation – because I am not having to think about the typing. In *Your Brain at Work*, David Rock gives an example of a quick email response that he has trained into his limbic brain. He has trained his brain to automatically use just three key taps to send a message that includes an emoji to clearly say to anyone who receives it, 'I've read your email, thanks and yes I will do that.'

Have a look at tasks you do on a regular basis. Is there a way that you can move some of the responsibility for how you do that task into your limbic brain by repeating it in such a way that you can do it without really 'thinking' about it?

TOP RIGHT QUESTIONS

For you

➤ What thing keeps popping into my head? If I did it now, would it simply go away?

➤ What is the difference between what I want to do first and what I should actually focus on and give my full attention?

➤ When was the last time I paid full attention to the person speaking to me?

➤ How many times today did I stop and think about my thinking?

➤ Am I trying to do too much at once? What could I delegate? What could I do now? What could I diarise? What could I decide not to do?

For others

➤ If you looked at your to do list and were really honest with yourself, what is the one thing you keep putting off? What harm would come to you if you spent just 10 minutes on it now to get it started?

➤ What is the most important thing you need to do today? How could you focus on that first?

LEARN MORE AND SHARE

Really great read

Your Brain at Work by David Rock

This is neuroscience made super simple. Rock narrates the day of a working couple in the story so that the science lessons have a real life context.

Blog

A short summary of the science in this chapter via a blog you can easily share:

> https://toprightthinking.com/2019/02/02/your-small-clever-brain/

Articles

S. Danziger, J. Levav and L. Avnaim-Pesso, 'Extraneous Factors in Judicial Decisions', *Proceedings of the National Academy of Sciences*, 108 (17) (2011), 6889–92.

PARTING SHOT

It seems ironic that a tiny part of our brain and its limited metabolic function is the difference between brilliance and barely getting by. But it's true for nearly all of us and we can't escape that basic biology – much as we would like to. Just telling yourself or other people to work harder doesn't cut it. Thinking better is the key.

We can train our brain to think better, but pushing it to do more than it is capable of without a rest or refuelling means that in the short term the quality of our decision making or our knowledge retention suffers.

Longer term, we are starting to understand that there can be implications for our mental health. Thinking about our thinking doesn't just make us more efficient at work or at getting our list of jobs for the day boxed off. The implications – and therefore the opportunities – of learning to think well are huge.

We'll do some more thinking about thinking in the next chapter.

EVIDENCE

There is a slight problem with
'data', 'evidence' and 'proof'

THE BIG IDEA

Have you ever tried to influence someone and failed, despite having a good business case with robust research and solid statistics? Were you stunned that they could not see things your way when all of the 'evidence' backed up the fact that you were right?

Everyone I have asked can give me an example of spending hours on a paper or presentation, checking the data and the resulting logical conclusion. They have gone into a meeting, assumed that the decision they wanted or the approval they were after was a no-brainer, and then received an entirely mystifying 'No'.

There is a piece of research on the science of influence that helps my clients enormously. It explains why, even when your facts are straight and your research is sound, people might still not see things your way. Why you can be 100 per cent 'right', and your data absolutely conclusive, but people *still* think you are wrong.

The research was done at Yale and it's a source I have looked into and trust. Interestingly, it was undertaken not by a psychologist but by one of the university's law professors – Dan Kahan. The research paper is quite long, so if my clients wanted a summary (before I wrote this book!) I used to direct them to an article I love, written by Marty Kaplan on AlterNet, If you Google 'The Most Depressing Discovery About the Brain, Ever' you will easily find it.

We dealt in Chapter 1 with cognitive dissonance – the fact that our brains are wired to pay attention to what we already believe to be true and disregard the things that don't fit with our view of what will or will not work. So we already know that if our brains are left unchecked, we will selectively listen and filter out things we don't want to hear. It stands to reason that this applies to other people too.

So far, so good. Remembering that if people you're trying to win over already hold a different view then cognitive dissonance may mean their brains unconsciously filter out what they don't agree with is undoubtedly helpful. But before you conclude that this explains completely and neatly why someone disagrees with your proposal or idea, and that all you have to do is find clever ways to get them to 'listen' properly, there is more of Marty's 'depressing' news to consider first.

The experiments carried out at Yale suggested that, if you have a particularly strong belief about something, you will not only filter out information. The news is worse. When presented with statistics that may prove you wrong, you will simply be mentally unable to do the maths.

Yes, you read that right. Faced with research you don't like, you get factual brain-freeze.

Kahan's research suggested that when people were presented with statistics that backed up something they already believed to be true, then they could understand the statistics and do the sums. But when presented with the same data to challenge something they didn't believe, they actually struggled to perform the very same calculations.

Because our brain wants to be right, it finds it hard to do the sums that might prove it wrong.

When I share this research, people often ask me about really excellent mathematicians. Surely, they would be an exception? Surely, they would actually still be able to understand and interpret statistics that contradict what they already believed to be true?

In fact, the research suggested the opposite. People who were better at statistical interpretation were even more impacted by this neural quirk. Kahan also found that, when presented with facts and statistics that contradict what we believe to be true, we tend to hold on to those views even more tenaciously. Sadly, until someone provides some equally well-researched project that contradicts Kahan's findings, it looks like we might be stuck with some science that makes life quite depressing.

Kahan's research was specifically about political beliefs, but it would be foolish to ignore the implications for influencing when stakes are high and there are strong opinions round the table. Particularly if you were hoping that your statistics would speak for themselves ...

Kaplan summaries the really lengthy paper pretty well.

> In Kahan's experiment, some people were asked to interpret a table of numbers about whether a skin cream reduced rashes, and some people were asked to interpret a different table – containing the same numbers – about whether a law banning private citizens from carrying concealed handguns reduced crime. Kahan found that when the numbers in the table conflicted with people's positions on gun control, they couldn't do the math right, though they could when the subject was skin cream. The bleakest finding was that the more advanced that people's math skills were, the more likely it was that their political views, whether liberal or conservative, made them less able to solve the math problem.

We all love to think we are rational and that our brains are logical and telling us the truth. You could choose to debate it all day long as a chicken-and-egg scenario – which comes first, the decision or what we feel about it? But I like to cut to the scientific chase and save a little time. The hard science and most of the research suggests this:

Logical thinking does not drive behaviour.
Emotion drives behaviour.

Smart people who have read the same science now think about their thinking before asking their teams to, 'take the emotion out of the decision'. They ask themselves what if their 'cold, hard decisions' are based on emotion *pretending* to be logic?

Leaders who are more open to the possibility of being wrong in my experience make better decisions in the end. Accepting that it is normal that our emotions come first and that we justify what we feel by backfilling with logic can help us to look more objectively at our motives for dismissing an idea or backing it to the hilt. If we are open to the possibility that we are flawed in our thinking and that our rational, mathematical brain might be playing tricks on us, we can look harder at what we see and what we believe to be true. We ask questions. We knows it pays to stay curious.

Emotions come first. We justify what we feel by backfilling with logic.

However, this is why the conclusion could be depressing – unless you are presenting to that quite rare leader – one who is fully and openly prepared to admit that they can't do the maths and doesn't know the answer – your hard work in creating graphs, research and numbers to back up your argument might fail. Even if you are 100 per cent right. Because if the person you are presenting to does not believe the idea is possible before you walk in the room, then no amount of data and logic will convince them otherwise.

It can also be depressing when you are managing others and you give them some feedback about their performance that they are not expecting and you think they might not like. I know from clients who have tried to have difficult feedback conversations that, even when they have taken the time to research an issue that has come to their attention and have some statistics or data to clearly illustrate the gap between expectations and performance, people simply may not be able to 'do the maths' when faced with difficult evidence about their results.

The reason I find this science particularly helpful day to day is that, without it, when we get a surprise 'No – I'm sorry that's not right', many of us would naturally question ourselves and wonder what we'd got wrong.

It's easy to think that you're to blame, and maybe aren't up to the job, but it might not be you. It might be that someone reading your recommendations simply has factual brain-freeze, and that their rejection has nothing to do with your gravitas or the quality of your work.

When you find yourself spending a lot of unproductive time ranting and getting frustrated that someone can't see your point of view when you know you are right, try to remember that your argument may just be something that others genuinely can't fathom.

The science helps us to understand that it is possible that even people who are smarter than you, might not be able to process your computations. Being right and having great data is sometimes not enough. Bringing that data to the table to show someone why they are not making the grade might not improve their performance.

I'm not sure that the research has neatly explained yet why this factual brain-freeze happens. My guess is that it is partly to do with, however senior or clever you are, you are still wired to be human. I'm thinking that if a finance director can't make sense of a presentation and they believe the opposite of what you are telling them to be true, that their Imposter and SCARF reactions might kick in – concepts we are moving on to in Chapters 4 and 5. But suffice it to say for now that, in their shoes, maybe you would use your seniority to get the person challenging you out of the door fast, rather than admit you couldn't do the maths?

GOT IT – NOW WHAT?

So, is it time to be depressed?

Well, I'm a glass-half-full person, so I think perhaps not. I like the idea that knowledge is power. And rather than keep this to ourselves and have all the power in our own hands, wouldn't it be really great if we could have grown-up conversations about how we think *and* feel? Maybe it would enable us to better critique concepts that are new to us and collaborate to come up with ideas and solve problems that previously seemed insurmountable?

The truth is your friend

My dad loves to say, 'If you can't hide it, feature it,' and I think the same could apply here. Could we see this challenge as a 'feature' of being human – and not something we have to strive to hide? I have found that stating how I feel at the outset of a conversation can put me in the right frame of mind to think more openly. My usual line is something like, 'I know I feel really strongly about this – so I know I need to be careful about dismissing what you have to say out of hand without listening properly. I'm going to really try to understand your points, could you do the same in return?'

Remember to remember

Simply knowing this science has made me more careful about making assumptions and cautious about dismissing something I don't think is true. However, I do have the advantage of talking or writing about it every day! Under pressure or faced with sums you can't do, it would be human to forget the science. Think about how, what or who could help you remember. A screen saver, a Post-it note, a conversation to reflect on difficult decisions you are facing with someone you trust who knows the science too. Anything that trains the memory to retain the research and remind you when you are under pressure that emotion beats logic and the factual brain-freeze is a real condition will help.

Name it

Share the knowledge with your team, your partner or your children. If we help people to understand that in an internal battle between emotion and reason, emotion will win (even if disguised as reason), perhaps that knowledge in itself can help people you know. Developing others to grow, change and be more open minded to genuine debate, will mean they will practice the skills – particularly when they are talking to you!

Grow your resilience

The research also suggested that how you feel about yourself can make a difference. If you are feeling confident about yourself in general, you are more likely to be clear sighted about when you might be wrong. So try to value your contribution and feel good about yourself before you know you are going to be faced with a difficult decision. An example in Kahan's research emphasises how important this can be.

Kahan conducted a follow-up experiment with people who said the economy was the most important issue to them, and who disapproved of US President Barack Obama's economic record. They were shown a graph of the previous year's employment statistics. It showed a rising line – an increase of a million jobs. They were asked whether the number of people with jobs had gone up, down or stayed about the same. Many, looking straight at the graph, said the number of jobs had gone down.

However, the researchers found that if people were asked to write a few sentences about an experience that had made them feel good about themselves, a significant number of them changed their minds about the economy – more were able to interpret accurately a rising line and a positive story.

It seems that if you spend a few minutes affirming your self-worth, you're more likely to be able to see the facts for what they are – and see a glass as half full.

Bide your time

Sometimes your idea will be both right and brilliant, but you aren't going to get anywhere for now. Think about whether you will be more productive doing something else, instead of reframing and pushing a policy that your boss simply isn't ready for. There's always tomorrow. Just remember not to tell them 'I told you this was a good idea a year ago' if they come round to your way of thinking!

Think 'brain tricks'

Some of the biases or tricks that we know our brain plays on us that we talked about in Chapter 1 can be in evidence here. Remembering those lies can help us to understand what is going on – and what you can do about it. For example, trying to influence a whole roomful of people where the most senior person in that room fundamentally and vehemently disagrees with you can be exceptionally difficult. The bandwagon effect, negativity bias and influence matrix might all be at play in combination. If the most senior person in the room can't do the maths, you now know why, but even so, do you think that person will admit it? Unlikely. How brave/foolish would the presenter have to be to point out their potential bias in front of everyone one else? Exceptionally. Knowledge is power, but be careful how you use it.

To stand any chance of your idea taking hold, you might need to think about influencing people away from the table. Who might make the most senior person feel safe enough to explore an idea that they fundamentally don't like?

It's sad but true that sometimes good ideas simply don't get off the ground. Instead of flogging a dead horse, maybe find another one of a different colour and breed to put your energy into. Knowing when to pull back as well as when to push forwards is a skill in itself.

It *could* be you?

When you are thinking about the situation and how to influence it, make sure you are not blindly being affected by the same brain quirk. Ask yourself if you are seeing the data clearly or just the data you want to see?

In the case of people who report to you, if you have some difficult feedback that is just not sinking in, maybe its their relationship with you that is affecting their perception? Would they be more able to interpret the data or acknowledge an element of underperformance if a third party was involved – maybe a coach or someone from HR?

TOP RIGHT QUESTIONS

For you

➤ Is focusing on this a productive way to spend my time right now?

➤ What would I do if I knew I was right, but people were never going to agree?

➤ What could I do today that would pave the way for others to see things my way in a year?

➤ What makes me so sure that I'm not subject to 'fact brain-freeze' or cognitive dissonance right now?

➤ How important is my relationship with the person I fundamentally disagree with? Would it be a better use of our time and energy to find something that we can agree on and to put our energies into that?

For others

➤ What do you believe to be true that might get in the way of you believing that my feedback is valid?

➤ If there a way in which we could trial this at low cost and low risk that you would be comfortable with?

➤ What do you think we fundamentally disagree upon? What do you think we are broadly in agreement on?

➤ What do you think you are currently doing really well? How would you feel about some feedback I have regarding something you could improve?

LEARN MORE AND SHARE

Blog

There is a blog you can share about this phenomenon at:

https://toprightthinking.com/2016/11/11/can-we-really-change-our-minds/

Articles

The full Dan Kahan study undertaken at Yale can be accessed at:

http://papers.ssrn.com/sol3/papers.cfm?abstract_id=2319992

The Marty Kaplan summary of logic brain freeze is summarised at:

www.alternet.org/media/most-depressing-discovery-about-brain-ever

Another quick article that you can share that is written in down to earth language:

http://grist.org/politics/science-confirms-politics-wrecks-your-ability-to-do-math/

PARTING SHOT

You might be right. You may have all the evidence to prove it. You may be certain that your evidence is not tainted by your own 'brain tricks'. Yet it is perfectly possible that someone else could believe that you are wrong.

Sometimes debating right versus wrong gets you nowhere. Becoming emotional and fixating on the unfairness of a situation where someone simply sees it differently can be a real waste of both your brain power and your time.

Spend more time and energy on the things you can influence. Be honest with yourself. You may have to learn to live with the things you can't change – even if you are right.

Well, at least for now...

CHAPTER FOUR

IMPOSTER!

Why you might be able to
sleep better at night

THE BIG IDEA

Have you ever worried that the challenge or promotion that
you have just taken on is a step too far? Have you felt that
sinking feeling that today is going to be the day when you
finally get found out? The day when the mistakes, 'creative'
responses and near misses of your past are finally going to
catch up with you? And everything you have achieved will
slowly start to unravel as you are revealed as a fraud?

If so then you are not alone. Research has suggested that
over 70 per cent of us sometimes feel this way. Maybe some
science will calm your heart-rate.

The technical term given to this (very normal) feeling

in 1978 by two American psychologists was 'imposter syndrome'. It is so called because you feel yourself to be an imposter – somehow living a life that you do not rightly deserve. That you don't have the skills and expertise at the level your position or salary seems to merit.

You may remember a Talking Heads song called 'Once in a Lifetime', which talks about acquiring a large car, a beautiful house and a beautiful wife and wondering how on earth you reached that position – thinking this surely can't be *your* car, house or wife.

It's a great summary of how imposter syndrome can feel.

In our house we call imposter syndrome 'running from the blagging police'. We laugh over a beer as we imagine an old-fashioned bobby, in a blue uniform with the buttons stretched across his chest, running red-faced towards us and simultaneously blowing a whistle. When he finally catches up, he puts a friendly but firm hand on our shoulder and puffs, 'Come on, mate! Time's up. I've been after you for a while! You've had a good run at it but it is time to admit you don't really know what you are doing. Hand back the car/house/spouse.'

I have had clients who have told me that their life has changed quite literally overnight when they realised imposter syndrome was a 'real' thing. It is actually a very normal and very well-documented way to feel – particularly when you have just taken on a new job or a new challenge.

When I tell my clients that research (and my own experience) suggests this is the *Number 1 coaching topic for senior leaders* you can almost hear their sigh of relief. That's because, for most of us, success is a double-edged sword – the more you achieve, the more 'evidence' you will recall that you nearly didn't make it.

Counter-intuitive as it might seem to become more worried about your competence as you become more successful is normal, think about this train of logic (based on research and science).

To succeed in a new role, you have to take some risks, not be afraid of a challenge and learn some new things along the way.

Often the best way to learn involves getting things wrong or failing and trying again.

Failure improves your instinct/gut feel for what will and won't work.

Failure increases your learning and then your 'gut feel' is closer to the mark.

You get things 'right' (or nearly right) more often.

You get more comfortable with the ambiguity of being 'nearly right'.

Your subconscious knows it's not guess-work, even if you consciously think "I'm winging it".

Because you are better with ambiguity, you take more risks.

Things go well and you get promoted for being 'right' a lot and for being comfortable with taking risks that other people won't take.

These are some of the things that successful imposters think and feel:

With a bit of 'luck' they can usually pull something out of the bag when things look like they might go wrong.

They get better at navigating 'failure' (but secretly they feel it was maybe only by the skin of their teeth and they will be caught out next time).

They talk about 'dodging a bullet' or a 'lucky escape' and rationalise pulling something out of the bag as an 'educated guess', when everyone around them is impressed by their courage and calm under pressure.

They feel a little uncomfortable that the big job is getting easier. Everyone says they are doing great. People assume they spent hours coming up with the bullet-dodging solution or worked for weeks on an idea when you put it down to 'gut feel'. You are quite blasé or self-deprecating and sometimes feel a fraud.

It is not luck. It's not guesswork. It is not 'gut feel' if you are thinking that 'gut feel' is a random idea or unguided thinking that appears from nowhere. Instead 'gut feel' is your subconscious getting clever. Your 'gut feel' is actually a sound, practical sense of what will probably work. It will probably work because you have had the benefit of learning from your mistakes and practising this stuff over and over again.

And there you have the root of imposter syndrome. People who succeed tend to have lots of evidence of failure and only just getting things right or getting them done. When we have a job we love and we are great at it, we don't like to show off – especially if it feels a bit too 'easy'. We get worried we are missing something. We begin to doubt ourselves and the self-criticism starts.

Which one of these has your brain used to convince you that you are getting too big for your boots?

'Being this successful should feel harder than this?'

'I'm not really working hard enough to deserve this success.'

'That was close. I almost got that wrong, I should not be so well rewarded just because it worked out OK in the end.'

'I can't believe I have got this job, I don't really deserve it.'

'Someone will work out soon that I don't know the answers and I'm just guessing'

Imposter syndrome thoughts are partly down to how much knowledge we have about ourselves, relative to how little we have about others. We see ourselves from the *inside* – we know our every thought, we know what was a guess and what was a fact. We count and remember every time we only just dodged an epic fail. We breathe a sigh of relief when everyone else believes our 'guess-facts' as the truth.

But we see everyone else from the *outside* – we just see results and maybe the hard work they appeared to put in to get that result. We hear what they say – not what they think. We see their upright posture and their smile, not their sweaty palms or them practising their speech over and over again in the car on the way into work. In short, everyone else is feeling pretty much like you do. No one is perfect at everything the first time they do it.

GOT IT – NOW WHAT?

I don't like to refer to imposter syndrome as a 'syndrome' any more when I'm with clients. It makes it sound like an illness or something quite rare. Now that we know it is part of the human experience for most people, I talk about it as 'imposter thinking'. Or, even better, simply – IT. I like to make it smaller and put it in inverted commas! I think it helps to put "IT" in its place!

Put Imposter Thinking or "IT" in it's place!

Here are the tips that I share with my clients so that they can choose not to let imposter thinking ("IT") get in their way. I hope they help you too.

Accept "IT" as a normal part of being successful

Success usually relies on taking a few risks. Without taking some risks we can't really make any mistakes. Our best learning comes from getting things wrong and trying again. So making mistakes, rescuing some near misses and flying by the seat of your pants sometimes are likely to be part of the reason you are successful … not evidence of the opposite.

Accept "IT" as an inevitable consequence of our brains not being wired to hear other people's thoughts

We can only judge other people by what we see on the outside, by their results and outputs. What they say and do. We judge ourselves from the inside and on our intentions. We process thousands of thoughts every minute. Thus we know intimately about every time we had a near miss, or whether something we achieved owed much to a good dose of luck or chance. There could well be millions of pieces of evidence that you almost got that wrong. But there are millions of pieces of evidence in everyone else's mind too. It's just that we don't know about them because we can't see into the minds of other people and their motives, only our own.

Do the maths – there are worse things to be than an imposter

Bertrand Russell once said, 'The trouble with the world is that the stupid are cocksure and the intelligent are full of doubt.' It can be very easy to equate confidence with competence. However, research suggests that 70 per cent of people suffer from "IT" at some point in their lives. If you are a parent, do you remember coming home from the hospital with a newborn and no instructions?

If only 30 per cent of the population will never feel this way at some point in their lives, then experiencing "IT" puts you firmly in the majority.

There is more good news. You have to be quite clever to suffer from Imposter Thinking. This is because the daft are too daft to realise their incompetence is real. The smart people are the ones who are astute enough to worry about the extent of their abilities. Two psychologists David Dunning and Justin Kruger (Professors of Psychology at the University of Michigan and New York University Stern School of Business respectively), published a paper in 1999 which confirmed what Bertrand Russell had already written.

In their study they gave people of differing abilities a wide range of tasks. They also asked the participants to estimate how good they were at each task. Put simply, the people who performed lowest, significantly overestimated how good they were. Those who performed the best tended to think they performed only slightly above average.

This has given rise to a term called the Dunning-Kruger effect – people who are poor at certain tasks, mistakenly think they are good at them and those who are the best, significantly under-estimate their ability.

If you want to get technical, it is down to something called 'metacognition' – how good we are at thinking about our thinking. If you suffer from Imposter Thinking, it is actually likely to be because you are smart enough to be able to participate in metacognition – that is you are clever enough to be able to rationally think about your thinking.

In a collection of essays published in 2012, Dunning summarises:

> If you are incompetent, you can't know you're incompetent... the skills you need to produce a right answer are exactly the skills you need to recognise what a right answer is.

If you need more reassurance that IT is 'normal', combine this with the evidence that a lack of self-doubt is common in people with particular psychiatric disorders. Clinicians estimate that around 4 per cent of the population are sociopaths and 1 per cent are psychopaths. You may have also heard about the research undertaken by forensic psychologist Nathan Brooks in 2016, where a study of 261 senior executives in America showed that one in five of them had clinically significant levels of psychopathic traits.

In short, if you feel like an imposter sometimes, relax and do the maths. It means you aren't a psychopath or stupid. That's the good side of the equation, right?

If you feel "IT" sometimes, you are in good company

Many other, extremely successful people feel this way too.

Take Sheryl Sandberg (COO of Facebook, who went to Harvard and used to be chief of staff for a US secretary of state), who says, 'There are still days when I wake up feeling like a fraud, not sure I should be where I am.'

Howard Schultz (chairman and CEO of Starbucks and one of the top 400 richest people in the US (280 in the Forbes 400 in 2018) describes how the experience doesn't diminish if you get more senior. Having known many CEOs over the years, he says that there are 'very few people, whether you have been in the job before or not, who get into the [CEO's] seat and believe, today, that they are qualified'.

It's not restricted to business. Maya Angelou, a hugely gifted writer who has won Tonys and Grammys and been shortlisted for the Pulitzer Prize, wrote 'I have written 11 books but each time I think "uh-oh", they're going to find out now. I've run a game on everybody and they're going to find me out.' There have been countless articles on this topic in the *Harvard Business Review*, BBC News, the *Guardian*, *The Times* … It's really not just you.

How to combat "IT"

There are some simple strategies that have really helped me and my clients. They might help you too.

- When "IT" happens, welcome it. It is simply evidence that, despite your success, you haven't got too big for your boots and your brain still wants to learn more.

- Accept you don't have to achieve perfection to deserve what you have. No one is perfect or the finished article. And if you thought you were perfect and you are in a senior role, well ... please don't do the maths because there is a one-in-five chance you're a psychopath.

- Realise that you can reduce the risks. You can set your bar lower so it will happen less often. But you will also be pretty mediocre – certainly by your own standards and probably by everyone else's too.

- Don't expect "IT" to get any better or to disappear with age or experience – another promotion or more success won't make it go away. If anything, you will just get more 'evidence' that you have been overpromoted!

- Actively work with smart, honest people who have different strengths from you. Make it safe for them to give you feedback. You can stop worrying you will 'miss' something because if you do miss something or people are doubting your abilities, they'll let you know so you can do something about it.

- You have a choice about how much power to let "IT" have. Remember you can only think of one thing at once. Do you want that one thing to be your potential failure? Or your potential success? Decide not to give "IT" head-space and energy. That energy is better spent reflecting on the facts that underpin your success and learning from mistakes going forward. Choose to spend your energy wisely.

- Focus on what you did when something went well, not just on what you didn't do. You don't have to have done everything perfectly for the end result to be good enough. Remember the 80:20 rule – it is likely 80 per cent of your success resulted from just 20 per cent of the effort you put in. Go back to some quick maths. Ask yourself, 'How right do I need this to be?' – if a 20 per cent result or even a 50 per cent result would get you most of what you want, this leaves you with 50 to 80 per cent of your time and effort free to invest on other activities.

- The maths question can give you some interesting things to think about: 'OK, if 80 per cent of my time and effort became free today, what would I choose to invest it in?' Home? Work? Future Plans? You choose.

- Help yourself and others by naming "IT" for what it is. Dare to be vulnerable when your instincts are telling you to keep your cards close to your chest. It will make "IT" less insidious and easier to laugh about.

- Use the 'worried' feeling that you don't know enough because you are 'new' to your advantage. Remember, you are seeing things with fresh eyes. Research shows that many scientific breakthroughs come from non-experts daring to ask a 'stupid question'. I love the podcast 'Stupid Questions for Scientists' because Dr Michelle Dickinson actively encourages people to ask what they may think are 'stupid' questions – because most questions aren't stupid.

- If "IT" pops up, congratulate yourself that it is probably evidence you are conscientious, reflective, smart, honest and modest. Would you really want NOT to feel it and be the opposite of those?

TOP RIGHT QUESTIONS

For you:

➤ What do I fear will happen if I fail?

➤ Will I feel worse if I fail or worse if I don't even try?

For others:

➤ Whom do you see in the media or know of who would feel the fear and do it anyway? Or not feel the fear and do it anyway? What could you take from their example that might help you?

➤ Who could do this better than you? Might someone who is less able than you try to do it? How would watching either of these people succeed make you feel?

➤ What evidence do you have that you don't deserve a chance to learn to do this task well?

➤ What advice would you give your best friend or your protégée if they were about to take a big step and were scared stiff?

LEARN MORE AND SHARE

Really great reads

The Secret Thoughts of Successful Women by Valerie Young
Despite the title, not just for girls! A straight talking helpful book by a woman who has made it her life's purpose to research and help other people with Imposter Syndrome.

The Psychopath Test by Jon Ronson
A funny and accessible book to find out more about what it means to be a psychopath.

Blog

A quick summary on imposter syndrome you could share is at:

> www.itsnotbloodyrocketscience.com/uncategorized/
> do-you-have-imposter-syndrome/

Articles

A short article that mentions Brené Brown, imposter thinking and vulnerability:

> https://changeyourmindfast.com/2018/01/15/
> avoiding-vulnerability/

A short 2017 BBC article on leadership qualities and psychopathic tendencies:

> www.bbc.com/capital/story/20171102-do-
> psychopaths-really-make-better-leaders

A quick summary of the Nathan Brooks, CEO psychopath study:

www.independent.co.uk/news/world/australasia/
psychopaths-ceos-study-statistics-one-in-five-
psychopathic-traits-a7251251.html

PS don't worry about the original article being 'retracted' – it was retracted in a debate about whose research it was – the result isn't in question.

A simple article from the BBC futures website summarising the Dunning-Kruger effect:

www.bbc.com/future/story/20121125-why-the-stupid-
say-they're-smart

Internet resources

Brené Brown is fantastic on TED talks. She mentions IT a lot in two of her talks, both available on YouTube:

The Power of Vulnerability and *Listening to Shame*

A funny podcast to help you see 'stupid' questions in a different light:

https://worldpodcasts.com/stupid-questions-for-
scientists/

PARTING SHOT

Feeling like an imposter now and again isn't evidence you aren't up to the job or out of your depth. Instead it means that your brain would rather not do the new stuff that it is finding hard (it's a miser, remember, and wants to conserve energy by doing what it has always done). So thinking to yourself, 'Oh my God, I can't do this,' could simply just be your cautious and miserly brain catching up with some new things you have asked it to do. Stick at the new things and practise them and, in time, the job you felt that was a stretch too far will feel 'normal'. Don't always listen to yourself – particularly if your brain is about to talk you out of trying something new. If you listen, it will have 'succeeded' in keeping you safe and comfortable – but it may also have talked you out of success.

CHAPTER FIVE

SCARF

How you could be dramatically reducing the performance of your people ... without realising it

THE BIG IDEA

One of the most useful half-hours I ever had was spent listening to a neuroscientist talk about a brilliant model called SCARF and why coaching worked from a scientific perspective. All very interesting as a coach, but it also added huge value to me as an HR leader. Why? Because it made me think entirely differently about the potential reasons for under-performance at work and gave me an entirely different lens to look through to find solutions.

When we try to get under the skin of underperformance we tend to look primarily at the person who is underperforming.

What are *they* doing or not doing? Is it *their* 'skill' or 'will' that is the issue? It becomes all too easily about *them*.

Whilst there is no doubt that it can be really worthwhile to explore the skill or will gaps of someone who works with you, getting 'under their skin' can be exceptionally time consuming. There is sometimes a faster way to get their performance to improve.

The science that I learnt about in that half-hour helped me to realise that looking not just at the skill or will of the person who is underperforming, but the skill or will of the person who is *judging* them to be an underperformer, can be game changing.

And, yes, that does mean 'It could be you ...'

This doesn't sound very appealing, I accept. When someone is really irritating you, or your reputation is on the line because of their results, the last thing you want to do is gaze at your own belly button. But this analysis can take minutes. It can actually save you loads of time to ask yourself what part you may have played. After all, YOU are in charge of you, and if you are contributing something to the problem, it can be much faster to change one of your own actions, to see if it makes a difference. Influencing someone else to change what they are doing can and does take much longer – if it works at all.

In the case of underperformance, it is worth doing a quick check to make sure that you are not doing something inadvertently that is restricting someone's performance by up to 80 per cent. That's right, they may only be working with

20 per cent of their thinking capacity switched on and fully operational as a result of your actions.

This is where SCARF comes in. The theory was proposed by David Rock, who has written some of my favourite books around how understanding our brain wiring can help us to be more effective at work. Look him up on YouTube. He coined the acronym SCARF to summarise the five main triggers (buttons) that when activated (pressed) by someone or something can set off our 'fight-or-flight' reaction.

I expect you're familiar with the idea: put simply, we have some ancient Palaeolithic wiring in our brains that has been passed down from our ancestors that makes us want to safeguard ourselves when we are threatened either by fighting back or running away. We can easily understand why our ancestors needed this to survive – when you live in a cave, you either fight the bear or run away, otherwise you become bear food. And if you are bear food you don't get the chance to pass on your genes to the next generation.

This fight-or-flight thought path has become very well protected in the brain over centuries, so even though bears no longer chase us back to our caves we still have the same wiring – it's just set off by slightly different stimuli, now that our environment has evolved. The SCARF model uses a simple mnemonic to describe the five threats that make our Palaeolithic fight-or-flight response kick in. These are threats to our:

Status (our role or place in the pecking order),

Certainty (our sense of who we are and what we know),

Autonomy (our ability to control our lives),

Relatedness (our relationships or how we connect with others), or

Fairness (our sense of what is right or wrong).

So, back to underperformance. You might be able to think of a time recently when you purposely or inadvertently pressed someone's 'fairness' button. You know they didn't agree with you about something and that they thought that what you were asking them to do was unreasonable. You knew the business required it anyway, so you gave them the hard stare and just told them to get on with it and stop whinging, right?

Well, SCARF helps us to understand that you probably have only a one-in-five chance of that working. At best. Because pressing someone's 'fairness' button also switches on that inbuilt fight-or-flight response. And by attaching sensors to our heads and watching what happens, neuroscientists have discovered that when that fight-or-flight response is switched on, the part of our brain that deals with rational thinking and problem solving is powered down. I really zoned in when I heard the neuroscientist make that link and I asked a question to make sure that the penny I thought had dropped for me was a real penny. It felt like it might be worth its weight in gold.

'Yes,' she said in response to my question to check. 'There is a direct correlation between putting someone under the sort of pressure that makes them feel threatened and their ability to think and reason. As neuroscientists we are confident that the brain's capacity to problem solve and think rationally is reduced by up to 80 per cent when a person feels under threat.'

What this recent science bombshell tells us is that, when you ask that colleague to do something that they think is not fair, not only do they instinctively not want to do it, but also they probably can't even process your request properly. Pressing their 'fairness' button diminishes by about 80 per cent their capacity to see your request in a rational way and to come up with solutions.

This helps to explain why that person who is usually so competent/helpful/creative won't be able to process and understand what you are asking. They certainly won't be able to come up with any solutions as to how they can get you what you want right now. They won't relate to why it is important to you and be able to rationalise it. They might not even remember the details of what you asked.

Going right back to the beginning of the chapter. When you encounter underperformance in someone it might not be *their* skill or *their* will that is the problem. It might be how *you* are asking for things to be done. It might be the fact that you have inadvertently reduced their capacity to think by about 80 per cent that is the problem. If you can adapt the manner in which you are asking for things to be done and change how your presence makes them feel, you might find their competence and enthusiasm return. Or even find they are not, in fact, someone you need to manage out of the business, but a potential star performer.

Remember, it doesn't matter if your request is actually fair or rational. Or whether you think you are being threatening or intimidating. You can't expect to change someone's innate response by logical argument when it has been hardwired for millennia. Telling yourself that you are being assertive and not aggressive won't work either. It's a bit like beauty. Threat is in the eye of the beholder. Arguing with them about why your request makes sense won't help. It will simply keep them in that place of fight-or-flight for longer. Pushing any of their five SCARF buttons, be it on purpose or accidentally, will simply keep their thinking capacity at about 20 per cent for as long as you continue to do it.

You might think it's an appalling bit of faulty wiring for modern life – and you might be right. But like it or not, when we are dealing with problems in our air-conditioned, high-tech offices, we still bring along a response in our brains that is literally millions of years old. No amount of clever business process or whizzy gadgets will make up for the fact that, when we feel threatened, our old 'reptilian' brain kicks in and makes us want to run, hide, fight or freeze. Remember from Chapter 2 that the brain's newer part (the prefrontal cortex) doesn't work very well at all. Given that this frontal cortex deals with thinking, evaluation and reflection, the SCARF reaction impairs our ability both to solve problems and to be aware of our own and others' feelings.

This science, then, might save you spending hours going backwards and forwards – asking people to do things, them not getting it done, going back and checking, even doing it yourself in the end. It might only take a few minutes of reflection for you to work out how to short circuit their wiring and get the response you need.

Given that threat is in the eye of the beholder, seeking feedback from someone who will be honest with you could be the key to making the people who work with you almost instantly more effective. Don't ask the colleague who is most like you, ask someone who is different from you – ideally someone who reports to you and for whom you can create a safe environment for them to tell you honestly how you make people feel. Understanding the biology/physiology can help both you and the person providing feedback to identify how your behaviour might be triggering the SCARF reaction.

Think about yourself. When you are not performing at your best and you start to feel worried about it, what happens? How do you feel? What do you notice about how your body reacts to a 'threat'? Think about a situation that made you feel you might fail and/or lose status in the team? Or when you last got some feedback and feared you were about to be 'found out' as an imposter (see Chapter 4).

When something like this happens, do you feel and look like you want to fight? (Perhaps you get tingling or sweaty palms, grit your teeth or go red in the face?) Or does your body go into 'flight' mode and find an excuse to get away from the situation as quickly as possible? (Perhaps your stomach churns so that you want to excuse yourself, you get a flush creeping up your neck that you want to hide, or your feet start twitching and you want to run away?)

These are all entirely normal reactions, which at a very simple physiological level all require blood and oxygen to persist. Oxygen is carried around our bodies by our red blood cells, so the two things are closely linked. Let's consider a flush or blush that may be triggered by feeling anxious or angry. In simple physical terms it is just 'evidence' that there has been increased blood flow to an area of your skin. If your heart is beating faster it means that more oxygen-rich blood is diverted to that area of your body.

The problem with our bodies is that we can't produce new blood and oxygen quickly enough to make those reactions happen without a knock-on effect elsewhere. If blood and oxygen have to be diverted to the place in your body that is hosting your reaction – e.g. if there is extra blood and oxygen at the site of your flushed skin or it is directed to your fast-pumping heart – it stands to reason it has to come from somewhere else.

Put simplistically, part of your body is starved of blood and oxygen temporarily in order to give you that flush, that tingle or that pumped-up feeling. And guess which area of the body is starved, and so switches to sleep mode and stops working properly? Yes, we have come full circle: it's your prefrontal cortex – the thinking part of your brain.

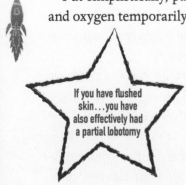

If you have flushed skin...you have also effectively had a partial lobotomy

So, just when you have been asked that really difficult question that has made your mouth go dry and a flush creep up to your cheeks, you know now that the rational part of your brain is about to let you down. Until your fight-or-flight response passes, you are unlikely to be able to think about the question rationally, or to judge how your blurted-out answer made someone else feel. Just when you need your clear-sighted thinking the most, you are probably at your most stupid because the part of your brain from which the blood and oxygen facilitating your threat response has been borrowed, is the very part that deals with logic, problem solving and an awareness of the feelings of others.

Equally, when someone is underperforming and you call them in to talk about it, how likely is it that you elevate their performance by pushing home your arguments when they go quiet and red in the face?

Put simply, it is not very likely that when you or any of your team feel threatened you will come up with your best answers, or indeed even be able to make sense of the question. You are not capable of being receptive to what is being said by someone else. Your thinking brain is just not working. You have effectively had a partial lobotomy.

The chances of a total human brain rewiring project being delivered in our lifetime are zero. It's probably a waste of time pretending you have 'grown out' of this reaction and telling yourself that you are 'too old', 'too senior' or 'too experienced' to behave like this.

I help my clients to let themselves off the hook by asking

what makes them think they can conquer, over twenty-five years in commercial life, a behaviour that has been alive and well in every human being for over a million?

People tell me that hearing this has changed their lives. They accept it is normal that they can't think at their best when they feel threatened – however irrational that threat might be. The flight/fight reaction is inevitable. The skill lies not in stopping the reaction – that is beyond us – but in retaining just enough objective thought to know the reaction for what it is.

I have helped people to train themselves with a concept called 'anchoring' so that when they feel their cheeks redden they can recall the SCARF acronym. Some of them imagine a pashmina or a Tom Baker as *Dr Who*-style stripy scarf at this point to kick in the memory. They remind themselves with the 20 per cent of their working brain that it is simply blood and oxygen rushing to that part of their body. Just biology and thoroughly normal. It will pass. They get better with practice at remembering through the haze of their own anger or fear that their thinking brain is not working so well. They vaguely remember that the temporary 'blankness' does not mean they are about to be exposed as a failure as a leader, parent, or partner. They just stop for a split second. Think SCARF. Then, instead of saying the thing that comes into their head from a brain that might only be 20 per cent functional, they have learnt to take a moment and take a breath first. This gives their body has chance to return the blood and oxygen to where it belongs and switch the brain back on. They then have a fighting chance of making sense and not saying something that could do lasting harm to a relationship. Or retreat and look like they are sulking. Or counter the threatening behaviour they receive with more of the same in return – and put their colleague's brain into 20 per cent functionality as well.

We repeat what gets rewarded. We avoid things that make us feel threatened

For all our high-tech living and our sophisticated conversations, human beings are pretty simple creatures. We move towards and repeat things that get us noticed or rewarded. We stop doing things and avoid things that don't get a reward or make us feel threatened.

Remember what they used to say on the National Lottery ads – 'It could be you'.

Sometimes people don't do what you have asked – not because they don't want to or are being childish, but because the part of the brain that needs to be working in order for them to operate just isn't. However talented or experienced someone is, they are unlikely to come up with an idea or be able to understand where you are coming from if their thinking brain is working at only 20 per cent capacity at the point at which you explained yourself. So 'it could be you' because either:

> something that you said or how you said it made their brain not work properly, or

> something you said or did is contributing to their underperformance.

It's a pretty challenging thought. I have reflected on some of my past roles when I have led big teams, and realise now that some simple things I was doing were inhibiting the performance of my people.

I recall making a decision on someone's behalf and sending them a quick email to tell them it was all sorted. I intended to speed things up and be helpful so they could focus on a big event. But I wonder now, did I accidentally make them less effective that day as they fumed about me taking away their autonomy?

I remember during a meeting with our senior leaders, I had asked one of my most competent junior managers to come along in case there were any technical questions. We strayed off piste and I passed the conversational baton over to her and asked her to contribute her ideas when she wasn't expecting it – I thought I was giving her a chance to shine – and then was really confused about why, when she knew so much, she could offer so little. I reflect now that I may well have threatened her sense of certainty about what her role was at that meeting. In this case I wanted to give her the opportunity to show off her knowledge and take credit for her own work. Instead I now regret that I probably made her feel exposed and embarrassed.

My intentions were good in both cases. I have come to understand that when I 'threaten' people it is usually with the best of motives. It would not have bothered me to speak in the moment about a subject I loved, but I made the mistake of assuming that another person would feel as I did.

What sets off someone else's SCARF reaction is different from what sets off yours. You may feel you have been 'firm but fair' when you have actually sent your colleague's brain running for the hills. What you thought you said to a team member may not have been a message they were able to hear.

Remember, 'It could be you'.

GOT IT – NOW WHAT?

The lesson I have learnt the hard way when leading others is that you need to talk less, listen more, watch and really pay attention. Even more so when time is tight, the stakes are high and you are in a rush or on a roll. Because that is when you will miss a creep of red scrolling up someone's neck, or see them tapping their feet or looking for the door. Listen to the challenge you do get back for any sense that someone's SCARF reaction has been triggered. More importantly, listen to what they don't say. I have learnt to beware of getting a 'yes' too quickly to something I thought was going to be challenging to talk about. I learnt the hard way that a quick 'yes' often was the fast track to me leaving someone alone – which was exactly what they wanted me to do.

Here are some things that might help you to reflect on how to help yourself or others. And for you to make it safe for people to give you feedback when you get it wrong.

Prepare before you challenge

Think about SCARF when you are about to ask someone to do something. Prepare to look out for any tell-tale physical signs. Pay attention if you get a 'yes' more quickly than you were expecting, or you don't get the challenge you imagined. It is easy to congratulate yourself for getting a yes and ticking something off your to-do list, but before you do that, give the person some time to think and reflect. Have something that sounds like you're ready and waiting for when this happens. 'It might be a bigger ask than I can understand, so give it some thought. Could we catch up in about an hour so we can discuss how you feel about it?'

Don't beat yourself up – reflect positively instead

You aren't likely to rid yourself of a million years of human nature, so rather than berating yourself for blurting out something ridiculous or untrue when you were in a tight spot at work or were having an argument with your partner, take a few minutes to think about what you could do next time and how could you remind yourself to do it.

Don't make a bad situation worse

Think about the language you use to talk to yourself about it. 'God you idiot! Why on earth didn't I say XYZ? It's so obvious, they must think I'm stupid. Maybe I'm losing it.' isn't going to help you to get out of your SCARF thinking and switch on your thinking brain. Use more positive and less judgemental question on yourself: 'What could I do to buy some time to get my brain back in gear the next time I feel myself going red?'

Have a well-worn 'get out of jail' phrase you can remember

Find and practise a response that gives you time to think at that point where you can barely string a sensible sentence together. I've found I can pull out – 'Great question! Can I reflect on that for a moment?' even when my brain is only working at 20 per cent of its thinking capacity. Then be still and quiet (people will assume you are thinking, not panicking). And *breathe*!

Be wary of making (or accepting) promises you (or they) can't keep

Hopefully you now appreciate that your mind doesn't go blank when the stakes are high because you are stupid (well, not for more than a second or two, anyway). It cuts both ways – someone who just told you a 'lie' in response to a challenge might not be being deliberately untruthful. Simply reading this may have been enough to help you remember that clamming up or saying things you don't mean under pressure can be simple biology. A friend of mine who used to be plagued with insecurity about her performance under pressure now accepts her 'temporary stupid brain' for what it is. A lack of blood and oxygen. Don't make your stupidity permanent by allowing your mouth to say something that your brain does not mean! And if you do, apologise quickly and explain why you said it. Don't compound the problem by creating a web of deliberate 'lies' to cover up your first accidental one.

Pay attention to your body

Be mindful. When I get tingling palms, something in my brain vaguely remembers a stripy scarf and something about blood and oxygen. Now, rather than carrying on speaking when I feel my palms tingle, I take a deep breath (to replenish some oxygen) and try NOT to speak for a moment. It takes practice but it does work.

Use what you know

A smart choice to save time and get better results is to find ways to give other people a minute before you get them to respond when the stakes are high and tensions are higher. Or you might spend hours unravelling what they promised when they had a SCARF on! Can you prepare them in some way by saying something like, 'It's OK. Take a minute to think'? Just make sure your body language is giving them the same impression ... tapping your foot or looking at your watch as you give them a moment is not likely to help them unravel their scarf.

Make it safe to say difficult things

I ask some really tough questions of my clients and I don't apologise for that, but I also look for physical signs of SCARF. If I see them, I know that, whilst I might be getting somewhere, I will need to adjust the rapport and be more supportive to make it safe for them to answer and to have time to think.

Mind your language

When you need to be challenging or to explore underperformance, ask questions that use 'what' instead of 'why' – it's much less judgemental and so less likely to trigger a SCARF reaction. Equally, replacing 'Yes, but' with 'Yes, and'

When you need to challenge, ask questions that use "What" instead of "Why"

can work too. However, do ask questions. Apparently being asked a good open question sends blood and oxygen back to the problem-solving area of our brains. So asking a question gets someone's brain back in the conversation.

Train your brain

Remembering these steps won't come easily. You will need a lot of practice to recall these tips because you are trying to remember them with a brain that might only be 20 per cent functional. There is a fantastic book by Dr Dave Alred called *The Pressure Principle*. Dr Alred has worked with many professional sports people (Jonny Wilkinson is quoted on the front cover saying 'Dave Alred is a genius – he changed my life'). In the book he shares how to take control in high-pressure situations and train yourself in the skill of getting your brain back in the game. He describes taking control of the adrenaline and energy you generate when you are in fight-or-flight mode and channelling it into fantastic performance. He is at pains, however, to describe dealing with pressure and stress as a skill that needs practising over and over. So just as Jonny

Wilkinson practised kicking the ball over and over, he also practised training his brain to deal with the fight-or-flight hormones that we all naturally create.

My own repeated practice has enabled me to ask myself a simple question when I am getting really mad and about to let rip. I ask myself, 'Dulcie, what do you *really* want from this conversation?' It's not a perfect question, but after practising it for years, it now *does* come to mind and it *does* do the job.

The influence matrix ... again

You might be thinking to yourself that this whole chapter doesn't apply to you and any underperformance you have in your team, because you are a great and supportive boss. Mmmm. The science suggests that, however 'nice' you are, the very fact that you are in a position of authority means that any question you ask is significantly more likely to trigger the SCARF reaction than if it had been asked by someone less senior. If you are a parent, you might have felt nervous going into a head teacher's office – even if you match them for salary and experience. Think about how your mouth goes dry when you see a blue police light behind you, even if your conscious brain knows you aren't doing anything wrong. Authority makes SCARF more likely. So just accept that as normal.

Get your head ready

One of the things my clients have noticed and fed back is that SCARF (and Imposter Thinking from Chapter Four) is more likely to happen when you are feeling low, tired or unprepared. The negative "can't do" mindset that comes with being flustered or exhausted seems to exacerbate SCARF and the feeling that you aren't up to the job. So if you have an important meeting coming up with someone who can catch you off guard and make you feel less than your best, make sure you arrive early and take a little extra time to prepare. As well as doing some physical preparation and having all the information you need, put some time aside to get yourself into the right head space. Deliberately adopting a positive mindset and getting your head in a good place can lessen the impact of SCARF and Imposter Thinking.

TOP RIGHT QUESTIONS

For you

➤ Is there a pattern? When am I most likely to experience the SCARF reaction? Does it happen more at a particular time of day, after a specific event or with a particular person or group of people?

➤ How could I use my knowledge about SCARF and the patterns I experience to help me to plan to deal with SCARF differently?

➤ What could I do to build a different relationship with someone who SCARFs me or who I might SCARF?

➤ What could I rehearse saying or doing that would buy my body time to redirect the blood and oxygen back to the clever part of my brain?

➤ What will I do if I see the SCARF reaction in others to take control of my own emotions?

For others

➤ What could you learn to say or do that would at least not make the problem worse?

➤ Can I share this science with you? [Explain SCARF] Would you be OK to let me know of any times during the past week where I triggered this reaction in you?

➤ Imagine the person who makes you feel this way is listening to our conversation now. How might they feel? What could you do with that?

➤ What can you do to put right what you said and didn't mean?

➤ What could you do differently to make sure people still hear your challenging messages but without the thinking part of their brain being temporarily disabled?

➤ Which part of you might like to some extent that you can exert control in this way?

➤ To what extent are you assuming their reactions are the same as yours?

➤ How could you get feedback that could help you if we assume that you do inadvertently threaten the thinking of your team?

LEARN MORE AND SHARE

Really great reads

Quiet Leadership by David Rock
This book talks about SCARF in detail and also includes some other great insights on how to use your brain to lead well.

The Pressure Principle by Dr Dave Alred
Easy to read and relate to, and full of brilliant suggestions and good sporting anecdotes.

Blog

There is a blog you can share that summarises what SCARF is at:

https://toprightthinking.com/2016/11/11/performing-under-pressure/

Internet resources

The inventor of the acronym SCARF is David Rock. Google him and watch him talk about it on YouTube.

PARTING SHOT

Some of my clients have told me that just knowing about the SCARF reaction has literally been life changing. When you feel the tingle or get reaction, just stop and breathe for a moment. When you see it in someone else, don't kick them whilst they are down. Give them a moment so you can argue with a fully functional grown-up – and not a lobotomised zombie.

When faced with underperformance, think about what you might be contributing to the problem. Are you absolutely certain that your team are firing on all cylinders with their thinking brains fully engaged? Before you reassure yourself there is nothing to know, think about how hard you might find it to tell your boss that they make you feel nervous or threatened. Very hard? Thought so. There's more help on this in Chapter 9, where we'll explore how to lead with a high-support, high-challenge approach. But for now, perhaps just assume SCARF might be happening. And don't do anything to make it any worse!

CHAPTER SIX

BE MORE LIKE ME

Why it's a good job that everyone is not
'a bit more like you'

THE REALLY BIG IDEA

When I look back on my early leadership years there are
times when I cringe. I managed my first large team of people
(fourteen direct reports who were scattered across Wales
and the Midlands) at just twenty-six. Most of them were older
than me. Twelve of them were men. One had a degree. In
short, we had our jobs in common, but in some cases very
little else.

About six years later, I had moved into a human-resources
role and got the chance to do a formal qualification in psychometric testing. You may have come across these if you have
been in a formal interview process or a career-development

programme. Most psychometric tests are questionnaire based. There are two main types. The first is to test your aptitude – commonly in verbal or numerical reasoning. The second is to give you some insight into your behavioural preferences – so how you make decisions or whether you have a natural preference for leading or being led. It was when I qualified in my first behavioural psychometric tool (Myers Briggs – based on Jungian psychology) that I had one of those horrible sinking feelings that you suffer when you realise that you've been getting something very wrong.

I had experienced a few successful years – both financially and in terms of some of my people progressing to bigger roles. I thought I was pretty good at identifying what teams needed to do in order to be 'high performing'. I thought I had made those assumptions based on 'evidence'.

What I realised at the start of my experience in psychometrics was that my 'evidence' was flawed. I had assumed that, because I had 'evidence' that particular ways of working were successful for me, they would work well for other people too. That things that were as easy as breathing for me were things that other people too could pick up in a heartbeat. That things I disliked and found unhelpful were universally useless. Mmmm.

For those of you who are not familiar with Myers Briggs, MBTI, Insights or any of the other psychometrics that are based on the same psychology, here is a quick summary.

Many personality profiling tests are based on the work of Carl Jung, an eminent Swiss psychiatrist who died in 1961 and who is cited as founding analytical psychology. He was an early supporter of Freud and his work has influenced other fields such as anthropology and philosophy.

Jung identified eight core personality preferences. He proposed that our brains were born 'prewired' to prefer certain ways of doing things based on those eight preferences.

Because those things feel 'normal', we get used to those ways of doing things as our default position. To give an example, one of the preferences he talks about is for extraversion, a preference for thinking out loud and discussing things – in effect, discuss first, think alone later.

Science tells us every action has an equal and an opposite reaction and it is true here too – Jung explains there are opposite preferences. So, in the case of extraversion, he describes introversion, a preference for thinking things over internally before sharing your thoughts with others – in effect think alone first, discuss later.

What feels difficult or uncomfortable for you may be normal and easy to others

The real penny-drop moment for lots of teams and individuals I have worked with is that the 'opposite' preference (which to you feels more difficult or a little uncomfortable), feels just as 'normal' to other people as your 'normal' does to you.

So, if being asked to listen to what everyone else has to say before you give an opinion feels really frustrating and leaves you itching to speak up, remember that being asked to speak up first and give an opinion on something when you have not had time to reflect first feels entirely alien to others.

Myers and Briggs were a mother and daughter who turned Jungian thinking into a questionnaire that millions of people worldwide have now completed. They define their core preferences as a four-letter sequence: E or I, N or S (iNtuition – because the I was used for Introversion), T or F and J or P, giving us sixteen (2 × 2 × 2 × 2) possible profiles. So, one person might prefer an INTJ approach to life while another adopts an ESFP one.

This is a very simple summary of Jungian psychology, but it doesn't pay to get too tied up in the science. As you might expect, we have made great leaps in understanding the brain and human behaviour since Jung wrote his seminal *Psychological Types* in 1921. I don't find it at all surprising that Jung's findings and some of the profiling tests based on his science are now subject to criticism.

However, my experience is that using these profiles as a baseline to start a conversation about why your brain 'wiring' might be different from someone else's can be exceptionally useful. Indeed, they have been career and life transformative for some people I have worked with. Hence, although I'm well versed in the theory, I don't really concern myself with the debates that go on about scientific validity. Suffice to say I have seen some real and meaningful change happen after profiles were done, conversations were started and some fundamental differences between people were aired. The shared language of Jungian preferences was just the starting point.

Simply put, describing and understanding 'preferences' as innate helps people relate to different definitions of 'normal'. We begin to understand that another person seeing

MYERS BRIGGS (MBTI) SUMMARY

Extraversion and Introversion (E and I)
Do you prefer to externalise what you think or feel?
Or do you like to keep your thoughts and feelings to
yourself?

iNtuition and Sensing (N and S)
Do you prefer to use intuition to make decisions?
Or do you prefer to rely on what your senses tell you
–things you can physically see or hear?

Thinking and Feeling (T and F)
Do you prefer using logic and objective means to think
problems through? Or do you rely on something feeling right or not feeling right in terms of your values to
guide your decisions?

Judging and Perception (J and P)
Do you want a plan early on that you then like to stick
to? Or do you like to delay having a firm plan and rely
on your ability to improvise later on?

your answer as 'obvious' is probably unlikely. This means
discussions rely less on 'I hate it when you ...' and more on 'I
think I understand why you and I approach this differently.'
Consequently, talks don't descend into arguments and people
don't come to blows. My experience and a healthy respect for

the science that came before and after Jung means that I am certain that the following are true – whichever psychometric you use:

➤ We can get some phenomenal results for ourselves and other people if we use this stuff to kick off honest discussions to help us understand ourselves and one another better.

➤ Once you appreciate that arguing with someone who has a different perspective from you is futile because they think they are just as 'right' as you are, marvellous things can happen.

➤ We can completely overlook what we or other people are good at.

➤ What you think is easy and take for granted (so much so that you might not even consider them to be skills or attributes) might be something that other people aspire to, find difficult and would not find 'normal' in a million years.

➤ Rather than be surprised that other people don't see what you want to do as obvious, necessary or desirable, be surprised that any of us ever agree with anyone about anything.

➤ To complicate things further, the personality preferences we were born with or developed in our early years form only a part of how we make decisions. Once we add in personal experience, bias, bribery and fear, to name but four, it's highly likely that the 'stating the bleeding obvious' might not be quite as obvious as you think.

Back to the source of my embarrassment. I realised that had made some fundamental and incorrect assumptions about the people who worked with me.

Because we were in a fast-moving pub and nightclub environment, I had assumed that the business would attract extroverts who liked to talk, socialise and be happy to debate out loud. People who would work best if they were out-front, in the middle of a crowd, rather than needing a lot of quiet time to think and reflect. A team who were happy to make decisions quickly, based on their experience and instincts, and get back to the floor. People who were up for a change of plan at the last minute if it meant more money, engaged teams or happier customers. And because the business we worked for was part of a large global plc, I also assumed that everyone would know and understand that year-on-year profit growth was a given. That they would have hard heads and good logic, when it came to the numbers.

In short, I thought they were just like me ... (ENTP, if you had not worked that out for yourself).

Hence my embarrassment. Looking back on it now, I know that some of my team back then were quite a lot like me. But what I also know to be true is that some of them were not like me at all. And even the ones I thought were a lot like me might well not have been as much like me as I first thought ... and maybe I missed quite a lot of what they needed to perform at their best because it was different from what helped me to perform.

When I am running training sessions about leading teams, I tell this story and repeat some of the consequences of my assumptions. Our team meetings were lively, robust affairs where we would often dispense with the 'boring and constraining' tradition of an agenda and instead would loudly and sometimes quite aggressively debate the issues of the day – often overflowing into a bar where the debate got even more 'robust'. There were advantages – the meetings were egalitarian, so my views and ideas were dissected and discussed along with everyone else's. Passions ran high and so did our enthusiasm for 'winning'. We worked hard and played hard and so were happy to make mistakes or upset one another and laugh it off the next day.

But I reflect now on the people I thought were my 'underperformers'. I could continue to argue that I was right in my view of them because financially they did not succeed to the same extent as some others on the team (remembering that we can always find 'evidence' for what we believe to be true and puts our past actions into a good light – see cognitive bias and post rationalisation bias in Chapter 1).

I suspect it's no coincidence that they were also the people who needed time to think before sharing an idea out loud, or performed best with an expected and planned agenda, or who found their feelings more hurt than they let on by the good-natured banter that followed them sharing an idea.

I'm less hard on myself than I used to be about my early years as a leader. When I cringe, I remind myself that my actions came from a well-intentioned place – I wanted to create a fun, vibrant team where I was a first amongst equals, rather than 'the boss' in a boring workplace where no one was up for a challenge or a laugh. I succeeded in some of that but I did miss out on some success that I am sure was there to be had, because I made assumptions about people. I thought they thought like me. In truth, many of the team probably just got on my 'bandwagon' – whether it enabled them to be at their best or not.

I didn't pay enough attention. I was, frankly, naïve. I didn't know this science then. So, it was just natural human behaviour. I would love to return in a time machine and create the same energy, but with the space for everyone to grow, think and perform to their best.

One of the challenges that clients sometimes raise is that their way of working is working, so why change it? This is particularly relevant if you are dealing with successful people. Even if they buy the science and can identify that they might be asking people to 'comply' with their preferred way of doing things rather than adapt themselves to their teams, they might not buy that they should change. Because, even though the science suggests the people around them might not be working to their full potential, the cash is coming in. It is 'logical' that the status quo is 'working' because there is 'evidence' in the numbers.

It's a good challenge. I usually meet it by explaining how I used that same logic. In those early years as a leader, in terms of the numbers and the metrics, I was the highest-performing area manager in the brand and one of the best in the company. At the time, I congratulated myself on being top of the league tables and on how much profit I was making. What I wonder now I know the science is how much profit I *missed* making. What the gap in the league tables might have looked like if I had done more thinking as well as taking some action.

I might well have been £2 million ahead of budget in one of those financial years, but did I miss an opportunity for it to be double that? Strangely, being successful potentially meant I held on to some of those less helpful habits for longer. Beating budget and being a winner made it OK to stay the same. I wonder now if actually I missed the opportunity to hit the ball out of the park and create the most successful team that ever operated a group of pubs? It sounds a wild claim. But why not?

We often think that if we change or 'give something up' we will get a different result – and our fear is that the different result will be a negative one. We will lose money if we take our foot off the gas and don't push the whole time. We will be less successful if we let other people do things we feel are a waste of time. For me, it felt alien at first to stop and reflect, to pay as much attention to feelings as logic and sometimes to stick with a plan rather than going with a last-minute flash of inspiration.

I would now say that having a healthy respect for reflection, training myself to listen to the feelings of myself and others and sticking to a plan (even when I am DYING to leave something unfinished and start something else) has paid dividends for me personally. And I have clients who have moved their performance from being pretty good to being beyond what they imagined they could achieve.

During many years spent working with clients in diverse contexts and industries, I have come to see that exceptionally well-intentioned leadership habits can sometimes get in the way of breakthrough performance. I think this was the case for me too. I had ways of working that seemed very natural for me and helped me to be productive. It was my intention to help my team members to become happier at work and more productive too. We all want to do 'what is best' for our teams and it feels right for us to help them by suggesting that they do things in a way that we know, from our experience, works for us.

And therein lies the problem. We persist in encouraging others to work in a way that we genuinely think will 'get them there in the end'. We aren't being patronising when we are encouraging them to 'speak up more', 'go with the flow a bit more often' 'or trust your gut feel'. We say those things because we believe they will help them. Because we know from experience that they work. What we forget is that they have worked *for us*. There is no guarantee they will work *for them*.

> We persist in encouraging others to do things that work for us... even if it won't work for them

I'm certain that almost everyone I have worked with as a leader has made similar mistakes with the best of intentions. We all try to create a productive and comfortable working environment using what works for us, and assume it will work equally well for others. And we miss entirely, that some of our team are screaming inside for a bit of peace to think. Or dying to get out.

GOT IT – NOW WHAT?

There are many different profiling tools on the market for teams and individuals. You may have done MBTI, Insights, DISC, StrengthsFinder, Belbin, The Big 5/OCEAN or a whole host of others. You may see yourself as 'Leading with Red/ Yellow', as a 'Refiner-Creator', an 'Extraverted Thinker' or an 'IL. Something ... P ... I think ...'

Given that I am qualified to administer and interpret a wide range of the available tests, people ask me which profiling tools work best. Which give the best indicators of performance or potential at work? Whether any of them are scientifically proven?

It's an easy question to ask and a hard one to answer. Scientifically speaking, The Big 5/OCEAN seems to stand up to the most scrutiny. However, it's not as accessible as some of the other tools and therefore not that easy for teams to use in real life every day. Since most people are looking for a very short answer to the potentially long and complicated question 'Should I spend my time and money on them?' I take a different route when I answer it.

For me, the scientific debate about the validity, reliability and replicability of the various tests misses the point about their practical usage – as well as sending clients to sleep in the process. In short, you could choose to spend thousands on completing the most robust profile in the world. But if you read it once, make some vague commitments and then forget about it because something more urgent comes along then its validity doesn't matter – it was still a complete waste of your time and money.

Conversely, if completing the flakiest internet profile known to man free of charge online as part of a training day means that you and the guy in Accounts finally speak face-to-face and have some shared understanding and a bit of a laugh about why you wind each other up so much … well, in my practical experience that is usually worth something.

It is slightly interesting that two of the main psychologists on whom many of the psychometrics in the workplace are based (Karl Jung for Myers Briggs/Insights or Marston for DiSC) did not actually create any tests to apply their psychology. The creation of tests came afterwards, leading to many different tools being available and each one claiming it is 'soooo much better than the others'. One could be cynical and say the debate about which is 'best' is based more on companies wanting to make money from psychometrics and good old-fashioned marketing at work.

Now there is nothing wrong with making money or marketing, but my point is, I don't think you have to shell out lots of cash to do every profile with the expectation that one of them will help you to find a silver bullet that will change your life for ever, or provide the key to unlock your team's performance. Just pick one of the main profiling tools and use it genuinely as a starter for ten and as the basis to have some interesting conversations. Don't see any one of these tools as 'the answer'. Any of them will give you a reasonable baseline on which to have some interesting reflections about yourself and to have a shared language with other people about what makes you different.

Here's my short guide to what the scientific bottom line is and what you can do about it:

Other people are wired differently from you – do something quick and positive with that knowledge today, rather than when you 'have time'

No amount of cajoling, helping or 'coaching' others to see things your way will work in the long term, if their own wiring and experience mean they fundamentally disagree with you. If you are their boss they might pretend to agree, but bear in mind 'yes, of course' might actually mean 'please go away'. Pay attention today to resistance. What does it mean? What could you ask to find out more?

Work out what small thing you could start, stop or continue doing to help someone else to be brilliant.

Accept it's fundamentally likely that people won't agree with you – and proving you are 'right' might not get you the best result

Even when you think something is a statement of the bleeding obvious, it is extremely likely that you can find someone who is just as bright and experienced as you who disagrees. I use the American systems scientist Peter Senge's concept of the ladder to help people to visualise how sure two people can be that they are 'right' even if their answers are very different. It can be really useful to explore the rungs of other people's ladders rather than get to the top of yours and use your elevated position to push their ladder over.

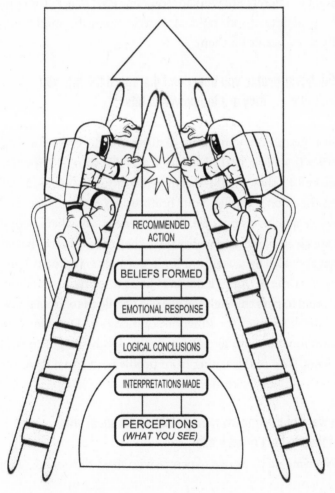

RECOMMENDED ACTION

BELIEFS FORMED

EMOTIONAL RESPONSE

LOGICAL CONCLUSIONS

INTERPRETATIONS MADE

PERCEPTIONS
(WHAT YOU SEE)

Be open to feedback that you 'being helpful' might not be helpful

'Helpful' just like 'beauty' can be in the eye of the beholder. What you think is a 'normal' way to behave, a 'rational' thing to think, or a 'sensible' way to plan, might work for you, but might absolutely not work for someone else. In fact, the complete opposite of your rational, normal or sensible might actually work better for them.

Whichever profile you use, don't disregard the bits you don't like ... they are the powerful bits

I love Cordelia Fine's take on this in her book *A Mind of Its Own* about how your brain distorts and deceives you. She writes that because the bad bits in a profile weren't known to you before, they should stick more because they are 'unusual' but they don't. Rather, your brain wants to forget the 'bad bits' as quickly as possible. She quotes a study where people were given a fake personality test – they remembered the bits that appealed because 'Your brain does not want to give processing time to things it doesn't like ... it seems it is easier for a camel to pass through the eye of a needle than for negative feedback to enter the kingdom of memory.' Don't let your brain fool you into glossing over the disadvantages to your wiring. The real learning from profiles can come from the bits that it hurt to read.

Beware of making sweeping statements about what it takes to be a great leader

It's normal to be drawn to people who share the qualities that we admire in ourselves. Look closely at any leadership competencies that you helped to develop. No doubt they have a healthy dose of you in them! Get them validated by other leaders who are just as successful as you but with wildly different styles.

If you do assessments for potential leaders in your business it will be helpful if your assessors differ in approach. If they're too similar, you will skew your results. Look closely at whether the process you are using favours certain personality profiles over others? I've seen assessment-centre exercises that only an extroverted thinker would pass, whereas a client being interviewed for a senior role in a huge global corporation recently was asked to submit a piece of written reflective thinking. Their interview (via Skype and by someone in another country) was based on that written piece of work. Clearly the HR person had thought quite carefully about ensuring their recruitment processes allowed people with different strengths to perform well.

Beware of the person who gives you 'all the right answers' in a job interview

Have they given you all the right answers because they were the answers you would give? If so you may inadvertently recruit someone who is just like you! If that is what you need, great, but I'm a huge fan of recruiting people who are very different from me these days. They get what I miss. They like what I don't like. They give me feedback I need to hear but would not notice without them.

Be careful of accidentally encouraging people to be more like you

Remember the influence matrix from Chapter 1? If you are the boss or are especially influential in a team, people will pay more attention to the things that you notice and reward. Remember the self-serving bias lie in that chapter, which suggests that whatever we ascribe our own success to we will rate more highly as a competency in others? Combine these two things and you can find that it becomes quite usual for people around you to become more like you – even if that is not necessarily a good thing. When we think a skill or behaviour that we have is a good one, we will more easily notice when others do it too and might even reward that behaviour. If we are the boss, people may try to copy the behaviours that

We can talk about valuing difference but accidentally extinguish the skills we don't have

they think we have because they know they are important and attractive to us. We can talk about valuing difference in a team, but accidentally extinguish the behaviours or skills that we don't have.

This also means that if your team know you have an introverted preference from a profile that you have shared with them, when they complete a profile they will be tempted to up their level of introversion to impress you – even if they are not conscious of it.

TOP RIGHT QUESTIONS

For you

➤ What have I thought is 'obvious' today? What might stop someone else seeing it the same way?

➤ What have I done today that worked well that I could do more of?

➤ What am I making excuses for not being good at that I could learn to do better?

➤ Who have I been angry with or frustrated by today because their priorities were different from mine?

For others

➤ What might you need to appreciate is easy for you but hard for others?

➤ In what ways might you be accidentally slowing things down?

➤ What would you do more of if you genuinely valued different skills to the ones you find come easily?

➤ What 3 things could you start doing right now to manage your frustration better when people don't see things the way that you do?

LEARN MORE AND SHARE

Blog

You can learn more about personality profiling at:

www.itsnotbloodyrocketscience.com/uncategorized/
are-mbtiinsightspersonality-profiles-still-worth-
doing/

Internet resources

Do a quick personality profile – based on your Harry Potter or Simpson's character best fit. Google MBTI Harry Potter or MBTI The Simpsons or look at:

www.16personalities.com/free-personality-test or
www.bustle.com/p/the-harry-potter-character-for-
your-myers-briggs-type-74656

PARTING SHOT

You can absolutely find evidence that some of the science behind some of the profiling tools is somewhat out of date and not 100 per cent robust. But 99 per cent of the clients I have used these tools with find *something* that enables them to believe that people thinking differently is a good thing. They begin to understand or are reminded that what they think is normal and obvious just isn't normal and obvious to someone else.

Understanding the natural wiring of other people by using one of these profiling tools can reduce your frustration with those you work or live with and enhance your relationships enormously. You also have a shared language to discuss some of the subjects that it might otherwise be difficult to raise – such as someone filling a pause in a conversation when you were using that silence to think.

What's not to like?

Just a word of warning. Don't be surprised when your brain resists adapting to other people and tells you that everything would be better if only people were more like you. It's a lie, but it can feel very real in the face of all the 'evidence' that you can provide them with.

LESS DOING, MORE THINKING

Short on time? Be smart about where
you spend it . . .
The power of reflection and working
within our sphere of influence

THE BIG IDEA

When I talk to people about their ambitions for themselves
or a change they want to make, the most common reason
they state for not having done it already is 'I don't have time'.
Most of us have used phrases like 'there aren't enough hours
in the day'. We would probably all like to press 'pause' on our
lives and for the world to stop turning now and again so that

we could get off have a rest or get things done with no interruptions.

We know it's not going to happen – but most of us don't bother to stop and think about where we are *actually* spending our time and what we are focusing our precious cerebral energy on. We keep busy and hope that we will find some time to do those things we are putting off – tomorrow, next week or – my personal favourite – 'when I've got a minute'.

We can sometimes be genuinely surprised when we don't find the time to keep our promises to ourselves or other people. We let people down by saying things like, 'I'm really sorry, I literally haven't had a moment free.' What I help my clients to understand is that this is a lie – the sort of lie we met in Chapter 1. Our cognitive dissonance kicks in – we can absolutely come up with evidence that we are telling the truth – that we indeed did not have a minute to spare. We can very easily show our honesty by listing and justifying all the things we did instead of the thing we promised to do. Unfortunately, that evidence can't be relied upon. Our brains are lying to us and we are just passing it on – albeit in good faith.

Let's begin by realising that when we say, 'Sorry, I didn't have time,' what we mean is, 'Sorry, I prioritised something else over that.' Or even more damning, 'Sorry I didn't want to do that, so I decided to do something else instead.'

Where it gets really interesting is when you look more closely into what you did or thought about instead. When you 'didn't have time', what was it that you prioritised over that promise you made to yourself or someone else?

Part of this reflection and thinking is easy. Your brain will look for all the noble and important things you did instead. You will find these come quickly to mind. What will be harder to ask your brain to find and admit are the things you prioritised that weren't so noble or useful. There are good reasons your brain doesn't want to go digging – it is trying to protect you from shame. How would you feel if your other half, instead of saying, 'I'm sorry darling I didn't have time,' was uber-honest with both themselves and you and said, 'Sorry, I was on Facebook for ten minutes this morning and I fully admit I put that ahead of booking the dogs in at the vets like I said I would.'

It's only when we reflect and force ourselves to consider some of the unattractive, useless, ugly, time-wasting activities that we did instead that we can truly make the most of our very precious hours.

Researchers at Harvard Business School took two groups of people doing the same job and asked one group to stop work fifteen minutes early and reflect on how they had spent their time that day. Remarkably, within just nine weeks, those doing fifteen minutes less work got more done. In measureable business tasks they became 24% more productive.

We are attracted to being busy. It makes us feel productive and useful. Stopping to think can feel like a luxury that we can't afford. This research turned that concept on its head. The researchers even investigated whether it made a difference

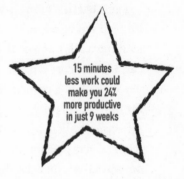

15 minutes less work could make you 24% more productive in just 9 weeks

whether people reflected on their own or whether they used that time to reflect in groups or with a colleague. The differences were not statistically significant. If you stop to reflect for fifteen minutes a day, regardless of how you do it, you are likely to see significant increases in your personal productivity. You should be able to do a quick return-on-investment (ROI) calculation. If you can show that you produce £100,000 a year of sales for your company, fifteen minutes of reflection a day should turn that into more than £124,000. If you save £50,000 a year for your company as part of your role, you can expect to save at least £62,000 if you spend the last fifteen minutes of each day thinking about what you did, rather just doing it.

Try multiplying that up. Imagine what could happen in your team if you have a sales target of £1 million. Or if you are set the challenging task of cutting your budgets or your costs. Imagine if stopping to think could deliver that for you with much less pain and many fewer hours worked late than you are used to.

Has to be worth a try?

I've tried this with clients. One director I have worked with for over ten years, swears by the ROI he gets from the fifteen-minute walk he now does most days before he gets in his car. He can cost what he has got from those fifteen minutes because he is a man who loves numbers and is responsible for millions of pounds' worth of them. He would tell you his reflective walk is worth thousands more to the business than what he gets paid for fifteen minutes of work if you divided his annual salary up accordingly. It's not often we calculate the worth of our thinking in this way, but it can help to convince our lying brains that taking time out to think is often worth much more to the business than keeping busy.

The real difficulty is not understanding the science. It is battling with your brain to put it into practice. Reflecting for fifteen minutes sounds like a great idea, but making it happen not just once or for a week but as a productive daily habit for the rest of your life is going to take graft. Most people fail to make those savings or those extra sales because they forget or avoid stopping to reflect because it is more comfortable to keep on 'doing stuff'. It is helpful to remind yourself now and again that our very human brains will convince us to 'stay busy' rather than to 'stop and reflect'. Remember your brain doesn't enjoy reflecting honestly on what you do, because it might not like what it finds.

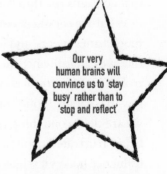

Our very human brains will convince us to 'stay busy' rather than to 'stop and reflect'

When you are reflecting, make it count. I like to use something called the sphere of influence to help people to reflect well (see diagram on page 156). I encourage clients to 'draw out' three circles one within the other, to use as a tool for analysing what they spent their time thinking about. They tell me that getting into this habit has really helped them to reflect well and to save time on subsequent days by expending their energy on things they can control rather than things they just need to learn to live with.

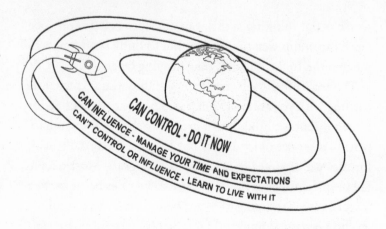

People invest a lot of time and energy in that outer circle that contains the things they can't control or influence.

What we should encourage ourselves to do is to spend as much time, energy and focus in the inner circles – on things that we can influence, or, even better, on things we can control. There are only so many hours in the day and, as we saw in Chapter 2, our brains are only truly productive when we are doing one thing at a time. Spending time and energy being frustrated about something that you can't control or influence makes it is likely that something exceptional which is absolutely within your control will not be delivered.

Think in real terms about your life right now. If you had only one hour, what could you do with it that would add real value or bring you real pleasure?

We do only get one chance to live every hour of our lives, but it is rare that we stop and ask ourselves, 'If I only have this hour once and I will never get this hour back, is this a productive thing for me to think about?'

I like to talk about energy. Everything we do takes energy. Thinking, talking, complaining, planning – they all take energy and time. Given that our energy and our time are finite, and we can only do one cognitive process at any one time, ask yourself whether the thing you are thinking about is a good use of your time and energy.

When I catch myself complaining about something I can't change or dwelling on something that is past, I ask myself this question:

> 'OK. So I've noticed I'm complaining about something I can't change. Shall I invest energy in that? Or should I spend the same energy on something productive instead?'

It's really hard to stop yourself in your tracks. Your brain finds it hugely difficult to accept evidence that you are wasting your own time. When your brain is on a roll, it loves to find evidence that it is right to be doing what it is doing. Don't be surprised if you find redirecting your energy hard to do, particularly when you need to do it the most. When we are getting frustrated or angry or upset, we can garner huge value from stopping to reflect and thinking about whether our thoughts or words are focused on what we can control, or on things that we just need to learn to live with.

In addition, don't be surprised that, when you do stop to think, you will easily be able to find plenty of 'yes buts' to justify carrying on spending your energy fuming inwardly or ranting outwardly.

Let's say something has gone wrong at work and you feel really mad about it. You will probably find it easy to list several reasons why it wasn't really your fault, why your boss is actually partly to blame, how the structure of the company is hindering you, or why an inefficient process is at the heart of the problem.

Your brain will find it quite easy to spend an hour venting to someone or seething inwardly about the contributing factors that you can either not control at all or only hope to influence. You are likely to find that a lot of your thinking will be about things in that outer circle of the sphere of influence. These things can be hugely frustrating, but they are not things that one hour (or a hundred) of invested energy will change at all. They are out of your control and influence. Frankly, the sooner you learn to live with them and find a way to solve your problem without dismantling the company processes and moving people who are in your way out of the department, the more effective you will be.

So, when you catch yourself and start to reflect in the moment, or when you take a planned pause for fifteen minutes to reflect, think particularly about where you might have wasted time dwelling, ranting or fuming. Split the problem into the three spheres: 1, 2, 3. 1: The central sphere. The parts of a problem you are in control of and should focus on. 2: The middle sphere. The aspects you can influence and the extent to which you can do so. 3: The outer sphere. The parts of the problem that frustrate you but are not within your control or influence.

Reflect honestly – where you spent time dwelling, what

could you have used that time for instead? Could you could have spent that hour having a conversation you have been avoiding but you know you need to have? Could you have focused on making one small change within your control that might influence the bigger picture later on?

GOT IT – NOW WHAT?

Do it now!

Take fifteen minutes right now (go on – before you tell your self you don't have time). You are going to think about an issue you have at the moment. Draw a three ring sphere of influence on a blank sheet of paper.

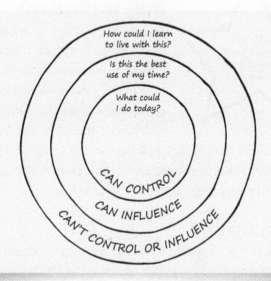

Write "can control" in the centre. Now note down all the things you could do personally that would make a difference to your issue. Include things you don't want to do, but could choose to do. Don't worry if they seem quite small items. Small things sometimes lead us to big places.

Write "can influence" in the middle circle. Note down the things you would like to try to change and that you may have some influence over. Reflect on how much time and effort you should realistically spend on trying.

Write "can't control or influence" in the outer ring. Note down the frustrations you have. They might be about other people steadfastly refusing to change. These are things that realistically, you may just have to learn to with.

Don't waste important energy pursuing a ship that has sailed

Think about the things in your circle – have they moved?

Sometimes we have to just accept that the stuff we are frustrated with in our outer circle could have been in our inner circle and within our control if we had found the courage or the time to tackle it sooner. If you can't change it, learn the lesson hard and learn it once and take action sooner next time. Don't waste important energy pursuing a ship that has sailed.

Don't lose sleep over it

It can be really tempting to skip some sleep to create a bit more time in your day. Whilst this could be OK as a one off, the science is very clear – even mild sleep depravation can lead to serious long-term health damage and mental-health issues. The neuroscientist Matthew Walker explains the science of sleep in *Why We Sleep*. This book has become an international best seller and rated as one of the books of the year in 2017 by many UK newspapers. Read it and the strong causal links he evidences to Alzheimer's disease, cancer, obesity and diabetes will probably put you off staying up late to finish a really important project for ever.

Beware of telling yourself that reflection isn't for you

A recent study by a Yale psychologist Gordon Pennycock looked at the connection between the Dunning-Kruger effect (that we met when thinking about Imposter Thinking) and our ability to be reflective. Pennycock found that those who didn't reflect believed they were performing well, even when they were not, because they didn't have the intelligence required for reflection and thus were too incompetent to accurately assess their own behaviour. As Shakespeare said many years before Pennycock or Dunning and Kruger, 'The fool doth think he is wise, but the wise man knows himself to be a fool.' (As You Like It).

Who do you have around you? Are they helping you to be productive?

We saw in Chapter 1 that our brains are keen for us to feel that we belong to a tribe, so it can be tempting to join in with group frustration in the workplace. Look for clues that you are spending your time and energy talking and thinking about things because 'everyone else is'. Remember our 'band-wagon' bias. It can be quite isolating to decide to focus our time and energy on doing something within our control, if everyone else is busy complaining about something in that outer circle. Think about how empowering it could feel to be the first to start a new 'tribe' – a really productive one. A group who are working on something that they can control and influence right now.

Have tactics to distract you from 'picking the scab'

Rather than waste hours fretting, venting and fuming (and we have all done), have tactics in place to prevent the 'picking' to stop it from being career limiting or taking over your life.

Do the maths Work out how much time you are spending on your core activity, what you want to achieve, things you can influence. Calculate in hours or minutes how much time was spent thinking about things that in reality you need to accept and move on from quickly.

Get it out Depending on your preferences try drawing your frustrations on a mind map, writing an email to the person frustrating you that you won't send or talk out loud to an empty chair. Externalising a problem can stop you going round in circles with it.

Permission to flag Give a friend or colleague permission to flag to you when you are not spending time productively. Beware, if you snap their head off when you are trying to fix something you can't influence, they will only let you know once.

Deliberate thirty minutes The aim is to stop your brain from ploughing on with something unproductive or dwelling on something for three ten-minutes sessions. The idea is that after those thirty minutes you will have distanced yourself from the temptation to dwell and have engaged yourself in more productive work. Set an alarm and time yourself:

- ➤ Tell yourself that you are going to put off thinking about something for ten minutes initially. Deliberately do something you have been putting off for the first ten minutes.

- ➤ When the alarm goes off, tell yourself that you will do another ten minutes. Set the alarm and do another task you have been putting off.

- ➤ Then allow yourself a fun ten minutes as a 'reward' for doing two tasks you have been putting off. If you feel guilty, remind yourself that doing something that makes you feel good for ten minutes is less 'wasted time' than dwelling on something you can't change. You should find that this helps train your brain into investing energy in more productive things.

TOP RIGHT QUESTIONS

For you

➤ To what extent can I influence the thing I am focused on? Am I investing a commensurate amount of time and energy on it?

➤ Is this something I simply have to learn to live with and think less about?

➤ How could I make this reflection time really count?

➤ What is stopping me from putting time aside to think when I know it will help me to be more effective?

➤ What things do I love doing that are causing me to 'waste' time and energy?

For others

➢ What would make it OK for you to think about this less?

➢ What could I do that would make reflecting for fifteen minutes a day into a permanent habit for you?

➢ What are you spending time thinking about that you know in your heart of hearts you cannot influence or change?

➢ Who could help you to make your thinking more productive?

LEARN MORE AND SHARE

Really great read

The 7 Habits of Highly Effective People by Stephen Covey
A famous book that deserves to be read for some of the very sensible top tips in it that are relevant to life as well as leadership. Because it's well known, it can give you a shared language to discuss some of the concepts.

Blog

A short blog that describes reflection theory in brief is at:

> https://wordpress.com/post/changeyourmindfast.
> com/283

Article

Gretchen Gavett, 'The Power of Reflection at Work' *Harvard Business Review* online:

> https://hbr.org/2014/05/the-power-of-reflection-at-
> work

Internet resource

A good TED resource on how to think about your thinking:

> TED-Ed, *Rethinking Thinking* by Trevor Maber

PARTING SHOT

Everyone on our planet has the same amount of hours in their day. Any icon you can name and anyone you admire (Nelson Mandela, Sheryl Sandberg, Marie Curie) all have or had exactly the same number of minutes available to get things done as you do. Saying, 'I don't have time,' is likely to be a lie that you are telling yourself.

Use reflection to think about your thinking. Research suggests that fifteen minutes of reflection per day will make you over 25 per cent more productive in just nine weeks. What would a 25 per cent increase in productivity mean for you personally? Do you want to ignore that additional potential that you have ready and waiting?

Identify the things that you can't control or influence that you are wasting your precious brain energy on.

Be courageous and tackle the difficult things you are avoiding that you can control and influence instead. What is stopping you from reflecting for fifteen minutes right now?

If your brain tells you 'I don't have time,' or 'I'll do it later,' or 'It's a great idea, I'll start it tomorrow,' then go back to Chapter 1.

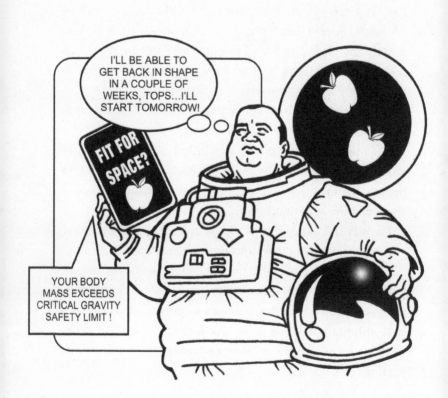

CHAPTER EIGHT

CHANGE IS IMPOSSIBLE

Well, almost ...

THE BIG IDEA

You have probably read somewhere that it takes between twenty-one and twenty-eight days to create a new habit. So, every time you have made a New Year's resolution in January it was a lifelong habit by the end of the month, right?

Erm ... Sorry, folks. To be fair, the myth of 'it takes a month to make a new habit' did come from science. It can be traced this back to a book called *Psycho-cybernetics* written in the 1960s by Dr Maxwell Maltz, a plastic surgeon turned psychologist. He wrote:

> It usually requires a minimum of about 21 days to
> effect any perceptible change in a mental image.

> Following plastic surgery it takes about 21 days
> for the average patient to get used to his new face.
> When an arm or leg is amputated the 'phantom
> limb' persists for about 21 days.

Maltz then went on to find 'evidence' that this translated into other situations.

Now as we know, if we set off to prove a hypothesis, our brain can usually find evidence that it is. And once we have a definite number in our head that came from 'science' it becomes fact, right?

Sadly not. So, a real bummer if you've just passed the twenty-one-day threshold in an exercise regime and thought you were home and dry. A much more robust and valid study undertaken at University College London in 2010 tracked people for eighty-four days to find out how long it took them to feel that a new 'health promoting' behaviour (i.e. diet or exercise) had become 'automatic' (i.e. a new habit).

They found it took on average sixty-six days for the behaviour to become habitual. So for every New Year resolution you make, it's likely you will have to persevere with it until at least 6 March.

A New Year resolution will need until 6 March to become habit

But there is good news. (Hurrah!) Another myth that the study quashed is that if you miss a day or fail a few times then all is lost. That was found to be rubbish. Missing a day made no difference to the creation of the habit in the long term.

Believing that it does is really unhelpful – it makes you feel you may as well give up trying to cut down your drinking just because you succumbed to a night on the wine in dry January.

Unsurprisingly, the average of sixty-six days concealed a wide variation. Even though all the people in the trial did their 'health thing' every day, it took them very different amounts of time to turn this into a real habit. One person took just eighteen days whilst another had not fully embedded the habit by the time the experiment ended after eighty-four days. (The team predicted success on day 254!)

The UCL scientists also tested how 'strong' the habit became by using a forty-two-point scale. They formed another hypothesis about habits – it takes less time for a simple habit (e.g. drinking a glass of water) to become 'strong' than for more complex ones (e.g. doing fifty sit-ups daily).

Rather than find a convenient generalisation that it takes us X days to form a habit, what the rigorous science from UCL found was that 'people differ in how quickly they can form habits, and how strong those habits can become'.

GOT IT – NOW WHAT?

Persevere

The UCL study did prove that as long as you continue doing a new behaviour consistently in a given situation, a new habit will form. But you have to persevere. It will take more than a month.

Be patient

At work, when there is a new way of doing something, it's likely that some people in your team will find it easy – they might nail it in a little over two weeks – and that some will struggle and might need support for the best part of a year. The UCL study suggests that both responses are 'normal'.

Remember that when you quickly assimilate around a change or a new process, it does not mean that everyone else around you feels the same. And sadly, if you are the boss and people see that you have it sussed and are praising those around you who found it pretty easy too, they are likely to feel really reluctant to admit that they are still finding it pretty hard ... whatever they might tell you. So just be careful about the language and signals that you use when you are encouraging people to do something new.

Make it automatic

It's worth knowing that habits are formed through a process called 'context-dependent repetition'. For example, imagine that every morning when you get into the office you decide you won't log into your emails straight away and instead you will pin up a Post-it note displaying a single achievement you want for that day.

The first time you do this, a mental link is formed between the context (arriving at your desk) and your response to that context (writing your Post-it). Each time you write a Post-it in response to arriving at your desk, this mental link gets stronger. When arriving at your desk prompts you to post your daily objective automatically without giving it much thought, a habit has formed.

Think about how you can support your team to create new productive habits. Until it becomes automatic, you can help by making the Post-it or other change something that you notice and ask about.

Imagine the future

Remember that our brain likes habits because they are mentally efficient – having a habit frees up the energy that we would otherwise put into remembering to do something. It's helpful to begin to imagine what fantastic use you could put your 'spare' energy to if you just created a new habit (say, defining your daily objective) and got a bad habit (say, wasting hours recycling email) out of the way.

Be happy – differently

It's true there are no 'silver bullets' to effect change. It takes graft. You might need to think about your good and bad habits in a different way. Imagine you are trying to stop doing something you really like, that you look forward to and makes you relaxed and happy – say drinking a glass of wine when you get in from work. Imagine that you are trying to create a habit that is 'better for you' by replacing that drink with something you don't like and won't look forward to (those fifty sit-ups again). It's going to be tough.

Look at what you really want and how your habit (good or bad) provided that. In the case of the glass of wine, perhaps you looked forward to it because it relaxed you and made you feel happy. If so, it's no surprise that it's a hard habit to break, especially if you are trying to replace it with something that doesn't make you relaxed and happy and is instead something you dread and makes your heart sink when you remember you've 'got to do it'. You will probably fail because your need to relax and feel happy after work contributed to creating the habit in the first place. Your brain will find lots of reasons to revert to the thing that makes you happy and that you like. You'll probably be able to find lots of evidence that your wine intake is OK after all.

You'll probably be more successful if you cut down your wine by replacing the first glass after work with something else that makes you happy, such as calling a friend who makes you laugh or indulging in a guilty TV pleasure. You might need to accept that your desire to do those sit-ups is never going to be strong enough to make it a habit. Would leaving your desk for ten minutes at lunchtime for a quick walk serve a similar purpose and be easier to turn into pleasure?

Choose not to die

There is a fantastic book by Lisa Laskow Lahey and Robert Kegan called *Immunity to Change* that I frequently recommend. The authors, both of whom are Harvard professors, quote a study where doctors told heart patients they would die if they did not change their habits. The study showed that, even when it was quite literally a matter of life or death, only one in seven of those people could change the bad habits that had threatened their lives. They chose to die instead. This is the power of the brain.

So being sincere about wanting to change a habit is not enough. Bad behaviours or habits are not generally weaknesses that are born out of bad intent or a lack of moral fibre. They are generally highly effective tactics that you have developed in order to protect something else – something that you really hold dear. Maybe you genuinely believe and have evidence that wine does help you relax after work. Or that keeping on top of email proves that you are busy and helps to keep you in the loop.

Use the Immunity Map Worksheet from the 'Learn More and Share' section of this chapter to map your resistance to change and see if it helps you to tackle your bad habits differently.

Remember your lies

At a subconscious level your brain is making some pretty big assumptions that are probably helping to keep you where you are. You assume that work will have been stressful and you will need the wine and – bingo – your brain keeps a careful eye open for reasons why your day was tough. (The 'why my day was stressful' stories will be the ones you tell your partner about over that same glass of wine.) Or you assume that everyone uses email and therefore checking it is the only way for you to stay in the loop. Can you find evidence that 'everyone' is communicating in that way and that you would miss the important things if you walked around the office and talked to people instead unless you really looked for it? Of course you can. There is plenty of evidence. It's just that you can only see the bit that proves your current view is 'right' (remember Chapter 1).

TOP RIGHT QUESTIONS

For you

➤ What is it that I really want?

➤ What will I have to give up to make room for those goals?

➤ What has made the 'bad' habits I have brilliantly effective?

➤ What is the inevitable consequence for me if I don't change?

➤ Does it matter enough?

For others

➤ If you knew that a daily 10 minute habit you would hate would add 5 years to your life, what would it take to make it happen?

➤ What "lies" are you telling yourself about your habits that are keeping you exactly where you are?

➤ What new habit could you start that could run alongside an old one and give you choice?

LEARN MORE AND SHARE

Really great read

Immunity to Change by Lisa Laskow Lahey and Robert Kegan.
I recommend this book to a client at least weekly. The techniques it advocates are not quick fixes, but they absolutely do work and are based on exceptionally robust research.

Blog

Here is a quick blog you could read and share with others. It focuses on New Year Resolutions, but the science is valid all year round!

https://toprightthinking.com/2017/01/27/broken-january-resolutions-create-better-habits-that-get-you-what-you-want/

Article

The research from UCL that I mention above is here to read in full:

Phillippa Lally, Cornelia H. M. van Jaarsveld, Henry W. W. Potts and Jane Wardle, 'How are Habits Formed?', *European Journal of Social Psychology*, online at: https://onlinelibrary.wiley.com/doi/abs/10.1002/ejsp.674

Internet resource

Immunity Map Worksheet from Harvard Extension School is at:

www.extension.harvard.edu/sites/extension.harvard.
edu/files/atoms/files/ext_immunity_map_0.pdf

PARTING SHOT

To break a habit you need to be both patient and kind to yourself. You must appreciate up front that it won't be easy (one in seven people would rather die instead). You also need to understand why a habit is there in the first place. It is likely to take time and effort to sit down and examine thoroughly what belief you hold that your brain is steadfastly refusing to let go of and how that might prevent you from changing something. Thinking about this upfront can help you to plan for the almost inevitable bumps in the road. Much of my coaching is about helping people to understand what is directly competing with their desire to change. What assumptions they are making and how those assumptions and beliefs are holding them back.

Good and bad habits persist over time because they are automatic and easy, and our brains like that. So the challenge for yourself and your team is to create some good habits that override some of the bad ones and stick at them long enough that they become tactics for your success. Like most things, if something was easy we would all be doing it already. And the self-help market worth millions and promising a twenty-eight-day result would not exist.

So I vote for accepting that changing habits is not easy … but using some simple tactics could make it easier.

TOP RIGHT

The problem with leadership

THE REALLY BIG IDEA

Most of the leaders I work with these days appreciate that telling people, 'Just do it, because I'm the boss,' doesn't actually work that well any more. Instead, businesses talk a lot about wanting to 'engage' with their employees – to 'empower' them and increase their 'autonomy'.

These are great words and sound aspirations, but what does engagement mean? Does it actually make a business more money? How do you actually *do* engagement/empowerment/autonomy on a day-to-day basis when the pressure is on and you work in an office with strip lighting on an unattractive business park, rather than having a trendy, bean-bag-filled space with a Starbucks concession?

First – the business case. Rather than just using words like 'empowerment' and 'autonomy' because everyone else seems to be, here is a quick rundown of the research. In a paper published in 2016 by Engage for Success called 'The Evidence: Case Study Heroes and Engagement Data Daemons', there were examples from a number of organisations that had been able to link engagement explicitly with increased sales and customer satisfaction. The Co-operative Group found statistically significant links between engagement and sales (sales were 4.2 per cent better in stores with high engagement). Marks and Spencer's found that absence levels were 25 per cent lower in stores with high engagement. RBS absence rates were 2 per cent lower and customer service scores were 5 per cent higher in engaged business units. Cineworld linked engagement with increased sales of food and beverages.

I have seen it myself. One of the employee engagement surveys that I was responsible for was quoted in an article in the *Sunday Telegraph* in October 2011. I wanted to see if I could make the link between profitability and engagement explicit and irrefutable in my own business. The service-profit chain theory isn't new and intuitively it makes sense to us that people who are happy at work will give better service. However, there is nothing like seeing those numbers link directly to sales and profit levers with your own eyes to make sure that you actually go and talk to team members about how engaged they are, rather than simply peppering your 'rally the troops' speeches with a few key words to pay lip service to it.

When I ran a series of engagement studies for 40,000 employees across a UK-wide business, I saw directly that higher levels of engagement gave better sales. For every one-point increase in the engagement scores, sales against the previous year went up by 0.19 points. There were other tangible benefits: guest satisfaction rose by 0.18 points and employee retention by 0.15. We also found there were higher standards of safety in sites where there was higher engagement. These might sound like small percentage increases, but when the business sells over 135 million meals and turns over £2 billion per year these numbers represent big cash opportunities.

There can be a tendency to confuse engagement with being 'happy-clappy' or dismiss it as HR 'fluff'. (Those who have been on the receiving end of me recently know I don't do either!) But importantly, having these assumptions in your mind about 'fluff' may mean that your brain overlooks the opportunity to pull a hard profit lever.

In a nutshell, higher levels of employee engagement make or save you money because you are doing two things:

1. Increasing the *satisfaction* people get from their jobs. This means they do the job well – even when you are not there – thus decreasing the investment you need to spend on managing them.

2. Increasing the *commitment* they feel to the company. This means they stay and perform well with you rather than one of your competitors, so reducing recruitment and induction costs.

Science and research help us to understand that getting under the skin of what engages people has almost nothing to do with HR 'fluff' and everything to do with using what we know about the human brain to get the best performance possible from individuals and teams.

You may have read about or been on training courses which talked about a 'servant' leadership style, or 'bottom-up' team-working. You might vaguely remember seeing some inverted triangles with employees at the top of the hierarchy and the CEO at the bottom. These concepts are not new. However, my practical experience has been that, whilst concepts and theories which seek to put engagement and empowerment at the heart of an organisation's DNA sound great, they are difficult to sell when profits are hard to come by or when times are tough.

To my mind this is because, whilst most of the books I have read about organisational behaviour and design cite business theory or case studies as the 'evidence' as to why we should try them out, they are easy to dismiss by telling ourselves that 'it wouldn't work here' or 'our business is not like that'.

However, recent scientific studies about how the human brain works suggest they *will* work. Given that most organisations are filled with human beings with the same evolved brain circuitry and physiology, it becomes very difficult to argue that 'that fluffy stuff won't work for us here in our business'. The science shows us that, irrefutably, these 'rules' about how the brain seems to respond to rewards or threats are common to us all. So, whether we like it or not, the research now evidences, through combining economics, evolutionary biology, psychology and neuroscience, that building trust, creating engagement and bringing the human side of ourselves to work are not 'nice to haves'. They are the first things a leader needs to do to get their people perform to their potential.

You have to have engagement and trust in your *organisational* DNA because the desire to engage and work with people we trust is in our *human* DNA. Evidence shows that we will only respond to a leader who is tough, strong, courageous and challenging if we trust them first. When we trust someone, our brain will look for reasons why that person's courage and strength are positive characteristics and how we could benefit from them personally. If we don't trust them, our human wiring will look for reasons why that tough and challenging approach might be a danger to us and something we want to avoid. We know about the pitfalls of that from the SCARF we met in Chapter 4.

The science helps us to accept that some of the behaviours that we learnt from our old boss simply don't work as well as they used to and why the JFDI approach (Just F***ing Do It) is either dead or dying. It's not just about Generation Y and millennials entering the workplace with different expectations, although a lot has been written about that. Science suggests that even when the workplace was staffed by with Generation X employees born in the sixties and seventies that there *even more* profit could have been had through increasing engagement, if we'd known then what we know now about how the human brain responds. Getting good financial results can make us lazy. Our brains are cognitive misers – a term we met in Chapter 1. Thinking in new ways takes up a lot of energy. Our brains would rather stick to the tried and tested methods of doing things. And if it isn't broke (and you are making enough money to keep your shareholders or owners happy), then why fix it?

Sometimes people only get to the point where they know they and their organisation need to change when the cash isn't coming in as easily as it used to. It is why a healthy chunk of my professional life is spent helping already successful leaders to tweak their thinking patterns, in businesses that are aggressively looking to increase profits or cash.

Engaging people is easy to talk about but hard to do

Some leaders I work with find increasing engagement and autonomy comes naturally, but I would say that the majority of people I have worked with at a senior level have come to accept via feedback or increased self-awareness in later life that they are merely 'OK' at it. The people I love working with don't cover up the realisation that genuine engagement doesn't come as naturally as they perhaps thought it did. I'm actually very fond of those leaders who are blunt and honest enough to confess they would still prefer to be completely in control of absolutely everything and would rather all jobs in the business were done 'their' way. I love their openness that they are learning to live with the discomfort of creating genuine engagement (rather than spending their entire lives at work micromanaging everyone). I love their candour when they make changes not through any sense of altruism or higher purpose but exclusively because they have come to trust the science and know it will make them more money.

The science and research around creating engagement and autonomy is quite easy to explain. However, science also explains why actually doing this in real life is easier said than done. Given too that engaging a team is only one of the many demands of a managerial role means that it is quite usual in my world for even experienced, talented and successful leaders to benefit from some help.

Remember changing the way we do things when they appear to have worked in the past takes energy that our brain does not want to invest. So I'm unfazed when managers go to great lengths to justify micromanaging their teams because 'We are just not that sort of business,' or 'There just isn't time,' or 'It just won't work because of the pressure here right now.' You are. There is. And it will.

First – the good news, the easy explanation. If you do a straw poll around the kitchen table with your family or in the bar with your friends and ask: 'Imagine someone asked you to do something that might physically harm you or that really frightened you. What would they need to do or say and how would they need to make you feel in order for you to even consider doing it?'

I have found that ninety-nine times out of a hundred (once you have debated 'How risky?' 'Is it life or death?' 'Would you do it for a million pounds?' etc.) that the same two things come up:

> 'I'd have to really trust them and their motives
> for asking me to do it,'

and

> 'They'd need to convince me they knew what they
> were doing and would stay strong and calm, even if
> I was panicking or things went wrong.'

'People are People' (as the mighty Depeche Mode appreciated). Human beings are human at work too. So if the only way for 'people' to get other 'people' to do something genuinely life-threatening was for us to a) trust them and b) see them as strong and capable, why would this be any different at work?

Think back to Chapter 1 when we talked about cognitive dissonance. People are people, and human beings would rather not do things they don't want to. We find compelling evidence for what we already believe to be true and will go to great lengths to convince ourselves that we really don't need to change after all. So in order to stand even a fighting chance of landing an unpopular decision in tough times, people need more from you than just a clear direction and a threat about what happens if they don't do something. People will question what you are asking them to do and justify not doing it in all sorts of complicated and time-wasting ways that mean you have to micromanage them to within an inch of their lives *unless* you can pass what I call the Double Test:

1. They must trust you as a person – they need to believe you have good intentions towards them.

2. They must trust your competence – they need to believe you are strong enough to act on those intentions.

The science and research suggest there is a pecking order. If someone's subconscious doesn't give you the thumbs-up to question 1 when people ask themselves if you have good intentions towards them, then they don't get as far as asking themselves question 2 about your capability. So you can be super-capable and have the most impressive CV in the world, but at a deep personal level people won't care because they

don't trust what you will do with all those skills and all that knowledge. In fact their subconscious thinks you might use your skills to hurt them. Your competence becomes a threat, not a benefit.

Leaders who get brilliant results fast in the toughest times pass this Double Test. When people ask themselves 'Do I trust them?' 'Do I think they are strong?' they get a fast 'Yes' to both. Those lucky leaders who are naturals and pass the Double Test quickly are personally highly effective because that speed of obtaining trust and respect means they don't need to spend much time 'evidencing' it. They don't need to remind people of their qualifications and experience. They don't need to wander round deliberately asking people about their weekends because they have been told it might help them seem a bit more human. This frees up time for them to spend on the business, getting other things done.

Researchers think that the key to getting this trust quickly lies in understanding our evolutionary biology. I find this a bit mind blowing, but I trust the science. Remember, some of our human wiring is really old – around two to three million years old – and researchers have found that some of this inherited wiring is still functioning and influences some of our thinking.

I can't really get my head around bits of my wiring being millions of years old, so I find it easier to think about our cave-dwelling ancestors again. Choosing the right person to be led by might literally have been a matter of life and death for them. Your ancestors' survival would have depended on being able to trust that a person genuinely wanted to keep them alive *and* was capable of physically protecting them and providing them with food and shelter. Pick well, based on the Double Test, and you get to pass on your genes and your subconscious behaviours. Pick badly and you die, and your genes die with you. So if your potential ancestor picked a leader who was strong, but who didn't see value in them as an individual, there was the real possibility of your ancestor becoming bear-bait or being left out in the cold if the cave was short on room. They didn't get the chance to become your ancestor because they died. Pick a leader who cares about you as an individual, AND who can fight the bear and you are home and dry.

All this is why we are attracted to particular traits in leaders. We have evolved with genetically coded behaviours that kept our ancestors alive. We sometimes don't stop to wonder what exactly it is that Manager A does to makes us brave enough to perform at our best. Or why we can't put our finger on why we don't like Manager B and take steps to cover ourselves. Some of the things we do subconsciously and without thinking are in our brain wiring because they were passed down to us from ancestors who survived. What the science helps us to understand is that it is not our super-sophisticated modern brains that are making some of our decisions about what engaging leadership is – some of it is our 'ancient' subconscious calling the shots.

We make decisions about whom to trust in a split second

Most of the time we make decisions about whom to trust in a split

191

second. The science suggests we made our mind up about people at most within seven seconds of meeting them. And after that point we will look for 'evidence' that this first impression is true.

Imagine someone meets you as part of a 'meet and greet' on the first day at your new company. You have seven seconds to get them on your side. Maybe you aren't your usual personable self. Perhaps you are distracted because you have just read the company reports and realise what an uphill struggle the next month is going to be. You are introduced and half miss their name or misunderstand the job they will do. They think you don't look like you are listening to them (you probably weren't). But the bad news is that every time they meet you subsequently, their brain will actively look for evidence that you don't listen. Worse, it will automatically deselect the times you do listen whilst staying constantly on the lookout for one time you don't. Using every ounce of energy you possess to focus on the people you meet for the first time and spending that seven seconds looking them straight in the eye, dredging up a genuine smile and simply appearing to be someone who cares about them as an individual can save you hours later on when you ask them to do something challenging. Their first impression – 'Here is someone I can trust' – will be the one they search out 'evidence' for.

The news gets worse before it gets better. Say the person is going to be one of your direct reports and spends a half an hour with you. Science has shown we give off around 800 non-verbal cues during that time. So no matter what you said, their subconscious will have absorbed 800 'clues' about you. Their impression is then likely to be set in stone. Give them the impression that this is something you are finding a chore and that you would much rather be 'getting down to business' is likely to make the 'getting down' to that business much more time consuming because you will have to work hard later on to establish yourself as a leader whose motives people can trust.

This means that we might well try and rationalise how we feel about our boss (or our prime minister or president) and be able to find examples of why our feelings are logical, but really, our subconscious brain has already chosen who we want to follow, way before our rational brain thought about the reasons why.

So back what can be achieved in seconds if you pass the Double Test. Listen in closely. Your team do more when you are not there because their brains want to look for evidence that what you asked them to do makes sense and is in their interest. You free up time to do additional things in the business.

When I'm asked for advice about why a really competent person is taking more time than it should to get a team aligned behind them. I advise them to get feedback as to why people might not trust them before they look to spend time and money anywhere else.

When someone doesn't trust you, they can spend a vast amount of energy trying to protect themselves from harm because they don't think you will protect them. So they triple-check everything. They introduce tick boxes to make sure things can't go wrong and you won't berate them. They want you there to check they are doing it right and to your standard. They would rather you tell them what to do so that they don't make the wrong guess.

The 'what's not in it for you' is that you have to be there all the time so they can check things with you and you can provide direction and instructions.

The fact that you might inadvertently be increasing the amount of time you need to spend at work cuts both ways – it is true of the leader who offers too much support and helps people to do the job. Even a really well-intentioned leader whom people love to bits might still not be able to stretch performance. Why? Look at the 800 clues per hour that they are giving people about their strength or capability. When you are giving people clues that you will avoid challenging conversations because you want a 'happy ship' and when you take difficult tasks off people when they struggle, you have the reverse problem. People need you there for constant reassurance. You have become like an overprotective parent. They like you there all the time checking in with them. Just in case. So you don't get to leave them to it and work on something else. Chances are you are doing some of the tasks they are perfectly capable of doing themselves to help them out.

In both of these cases we are inadvertently spending more time than we need to at work, either by micromanaging or nurturing. Equally, we are accidentally encouraging people not to perform to their potential. Where we are providing too much reassurance that 'It's OK' when people fail to complete a task on time and to a standard, we are actually helping them to believe that underperformance is OK. On the other hand, when people fear failure, they won't experiment and try new things. In micromanaging and over-checking we encourage people to do enough to not get shouted at – but no more.

The research and science builds a compelling case that you need both strength and trust to lead well. It is the two qualities in *combination* that are required to lead well and to build an autonomous team who can manage perfectly well without you. You need to be trusted as a person (so they feel they can try without fear when you aren't there) and perceived as strong (so they want to impress you and feel you can protect them if they get it wrong). The evidence suggests you can't lead to your potential if you have one and not the other.

Getting feedback about trust and strength is the first thing that I do when I'm asked to help a team or a leader where the performance is not where it should be, given the talent present. I use it particularly when performance seems to drop off when the leader is not there to 'supervise' the team. So if your people continually don't do things to the standard that you wanted or seem to drift away from their objectives when you are not there, you may have to face an uncomfortable truth. It is possible that their subconscious gave you a big red *Britain's Got Talent* 'X' buzzer to those fundamental questions about trusting your intentions and your capability. I have helped clients where we have had to face a very difficult truth. That this has been going on for years because their team have been looking for evidence that they didn't really trust them since they first met.

This all goes on at a subconscious level. We often miss what we did or didn't do to get the red 'X' and the buzzer. As usual there is more bad news before it gets better. Whilst you might get feedback about this sort of thing, your team may never tell you straight. For a start, they might not be able to put their finger on why they don't trust you. It's just a feeling they have. So they are unlikely to disclose something they can't back up with evidence. Even more fundamental than that, imagine telling someone more senior than you that fundamentally you don't trust their personal intentions … Mmm maybe not!

Back to the research. Some people don't like my choice of words – 'trust' and 'strength'. That's fine. Different experts describe these two key traits or dichotomies of 'trusting someone's good intentions' and 'believing someone has strong capability' using different terms, but all broadly find the same thing.

Stanford psychologist and professor Deborah Gruenfeld, in a number of academic papers and, more helpfully for us, really eloquently on YouTube, describes the two traits as 'approachability' and 'authority' – 'I will move towards you because I trust your intentions and I'm happy for you to be in authority because you know what you are doing and will be strong enough to do it.'

Harvard's Amy Cuddy talks about the dichotomies as 'warmth' and 'strength'. 'I warm to you because I trust your intentions,' 'I will follow you because you are strong and have the capability to protect me when things get tough.' You can read a summary in a *Harvard Business Review* article called 'Connect, Then Lead'.

Others who have translated this into practical advice describe 'support' and 'challenge'. 'You provide me with support, so I trust you care about me, and you challenge me because you are strong and know a lot and I'm OK with this.'

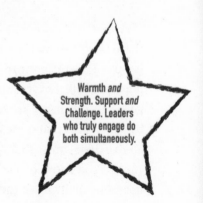

Warmth *and* Strength. Support *and* Challenge. Leaders who truly engage do both simultaneously.

OK. So, in principle this all makes sense and lots of separate research agrees. However, as I mentioned earlier, getting the idea is quite easy, but it is really hard to get right in practice. The reason for this is quite simple: like patting your head and circling your stomach, the two things are easy to do separately, but difficult to do together. In fact, let me rephrase that.

Our body and brain find it almost impossible to be both supportive and challenging at the same time.

Deborah Gruenfeld explains this well. To be authoritative, you need to project your experience and your knowledge as being greater than that of your team and to some extent this leads to distancing yourself from them. Then, to be approachable, you need to get closer to them and demonstrate genuine warmth and empathy – really valuing your relationships with people and hearing their perspective. Difficult to do both things at once.

Amy Cuddy and the Harvard team point out too that there is a hormonal correlation – feeling 'warm/supporting people' generally means that they and we are secreting a hormone called oxytocin. Feeling 'strong/being challenging' generally means we are secreting testosterone. The bad news biologically is that these two hormones are not very good at co-existing. Some evidence suggests that releasing oxytocin cancels out some of the testosterone and vice versa. Each hormone neutralises the power of the other. This helps to explain why it doesn't 'feel' right to do both together – our bodies have a biological issue with it. So even if your brain buys the idea that it makes good business sense and you get the science, don't be surprised if, at the very moment when you need to turn on both your warmth and your strength at the same time, your body and your brain (it is lazy, remember) resists.

What I see and hear described a lot is that trying to exhibit trust and strength at the same time is a bit like being on a see-saw. When one quality is high and visible, the other is probably low and hard to see.

This means that on some days, your people are pretty sure they can trust you because you genuinely seem to care, but other days you are more challenging and the last thing you seem is caring. One day you are hosting a conference and talking about autonomy, engagement and empowerment and you have a great time with your team being sociable in the evening, then later in the week you haul them all in and tell them to JFDI and cut expenses because the company needs to hit its monthly cash target. You might be able to convince yourself that you are doing both. You will be able to 'evidence' that you have done things that week both to build trust and to be strong and challenging – but because you haven't done them at the same time, you don't get the business benefits that deeper engagement and autonomy are capable of creating for you.

In summary:

1. Being a good leader is easy to describe: 'it takes warmth and strength'. But it is really difficult to do in practice because it requires you to do two different things at once and your body and brain don't like it. You need to work at it. The engagement and autonomy it creates, even when you are not in the room, will mean you can spend less time 'managing people', leaving you more time to focus on growing your business.

2. It is not likely that you can expect yourself or other people to 'grow up' and get over needing human warmth at work, because the impulse to want to trust and be protected is an inbuilt, protective bit of wiring that is millions of years old.

3. If people don't trust you, you will have to be a very present leader who has to check everything. People will be too scared of getting it wrong to invest much time and energy into doing it without you.

4. If people trust and like you, you have to keep challenging them, otherwise they get cosy, bored and don't perform well. Nice and comfy means more time at work for you because people like your reassurance. You have to chivvy them up and cheer them along to get anything done.

GOT IT – NOW WHAT?

First things first

Remember, research shows the two dichotomies have a pecking order. If people don't warm to you and trust you, then they probably won't think you are capable. Patrick Lencioni in his New York Times Best Seller *The Five Disfunctions of a Team*, describes trust as the first and fundamental thing that must exist between people in order for a team to function at all. Every piece of evidence I have been able to find suggests that without trust as a foundation, you can't build any relationships that are substantial and lasting. It would be like creating an architecturally fabulous house that is beautifully decorated on a bed of sand. No matter how good it looks, it's going to fall over. This means it makes sense to work on people trusting your intentions first. Think more simply about how your team could warm to you. Are you 'real' and authentic in your dealings with them? Are you 'likeable'?

Maybe you are trying to help another leader to become more effective and get the response 'I'm not here to be liked, I'm here to be respected.' A practical thing that I do is introduce people to research undertaken by leadership company Zenger Folkman. People were asked to rate their previous leaders across two scales – whether they liked them and whether they thought they were effective leaders. The study created a database of almost 52,000 leaders. Of those 52,000 people, only twenty-seven who were 'disliked' were also rated as 'effective'. Do the maths. It means only 0.05 per cent of the people who were not liked managed to convince people they were good at their job.

Even if you have heard a leader say they are 'not here to be liked' and 'don't have time for all that soft stuff', letting them read this research helps them to think about whether they want to persist with the assertions against those kind of odds. You may have noticed that employment references given these days stick to the barest of facts – what dates someone was employed from and to and in which role. The HR professional in me could talk you through the case law that makes that necessary these days. However, for our purposes in relation to the notion of being 'liked', it is much more probable that people will use their social networks to speak to people, rather than rely on a written reference from a former employer. Thus, it's pretty likely that people will phone someone up to ask 'What do you think of such and such?'

It is also a very regular topic at the coffee machine and over lunch. If people don't like you, it can affect the internal and external perception of your ability to do your job. So the leader you are helping with might well 'not be there to be liked' but they might be more likely to be more personable if they knew there was a clear correlation between being 'liked' with people saying, 'I actually don't think they are very good at their job.' The work of Zenger Folkman, which is widely cited in journals and magazines, explains succinctly why you need to be both liked *and* respected – not one or the other.

Use the 'evidence' to your advantage

We've covered ad infinitum that our brains look for evidence for what we already believe to be true. If we don't like or trust someone and we can't put our finger on why, we will try to find logical and more 'business-like' reasons to evidence why it's true. Use this to your advantage. Work on being trust-worthy first. People are then much more likely to look for evidence that you are good at your job and share that evidence when they are asked what they think about you.

Use a personality profiling tool

As we discussed in Chapter 6, there are a large number tools on the market such as Myers Briggs, Wave, Insights and so on. Most of them should help you to understand whether you will find the 'strength muscle' or the 'warmth' one easier to use. You can then plan with a coach or your HR support how to authentically develop the muscle that naturally gets used less.

Get some quality feedback

This is really difficult. If people don't trust you, they are likely to be too scared of the consequences to give you feedback. If they like you but don't believe you are that strong, they won't want to hurt your feelings by being critical. However there will always be clues hidden within your feedback and you can tune into those – if you really want to find them.

Try this. Write down two columns and put 'Warm' at the top of one and 'Strong' at the top of the other. Take the key words written down in your performance review or 360 feedback and put them into one of those columns. So 'helpful', 'genuine', 'tries' would probably go under the 'Warm' column. 'Driven', 'focused' and 'strive' would go under 'Strong'. Compare the columns. If you have a balance of words in both, you might be OK. If you have a long list in one column and next to nothing in the other, you might want to make it safe for someone to help you to understand what that means for you. Is it hiding a fundamental lack of trust, or do your team like you but think you are a bit of a pushover and are actually rather bored?

Be honest with yourself

Ask yourself what your intentions are towards your team. Do you really and deeply care if they succeed? Would you protect them? Would you trust 'you'?

If the answer is 'No' then they can probably sense it. Even if you talk a good game and tell them 'You can trust me,' they probably don't. No amount of telling them to trust you will make it any better – they will just look for evidence that it's a ploy for you to get something done.

Equally, ask yourself how strong you are when things aren't going well. Do you avoid difficult conversations because you don't want to upset people? Do you use language that signals strength and courage? Do you speak up for your team, even when someone much more senior than you challenges one of them unfairly?

If the answer is 'No' then you might have a great team spirit, but it might be too cosy for people to perform at their best. Being trustworthy but not challenging them might mean that you need to face facts – your team members might never achieve what they could whilst they continue to work for you. Can you live with that?

Fake it until you make it – but be careful

This is a tricky one. There was a brilliant BBC *Horizon* programme on the science of laughter. It highlighted that the brain releases different chemicals when people hear a real laugh versus a fake one. When we hear a genuine laugh, we warm to the person – and release chemicals that encourage us to move closer to them and trust them more. When we hear a fake laugh we release chemicals that make us suspicious and encourage us to create more distance between us and the other person. Worse still for those faking it, our brains order the release of chemicals in milliseconds, much less time than it would take to say 'fake laugh' or 'real laugh'. So people have moved away or towards you many seconds before their conscious brain has worked out whether you are being nice for real.

So if you don't actually care what people did at the weekend, you might be better off not touring the office on a Monday morning to ask them about it. They will sense you are faking it. Do walk around the office, but do so with the clever part of your brain fully switched on to 'curious' rather than going, 'I'd better ask about their weekend … oops bored already.' You will do more harm than good. Ask questions to get to know your team. Find genuine common ground and ways to like them as people. It might take a bit longer, but you will get far more time back if your people sense you are being genuine.

Remember, if you find your brain telling you it feels like you are wasting time on 'idle chit-chat', remind your head that giving people 'evidence'to like you could be the most productive thing you do all day.

Practise in real life, on real things

Take a piece of paper. Draw an L shaped axis. Draw an upright cross in the centre to fill the space and create four boxes.

1. Write down the leftmost vertical axis 'Trust/Support/Warmth'.

2. Write under the lower horizontal axis 'Strong/Challenging/Tough'.

3. Write 'Low' in the bottom left-hand corner.

4. Write 'High' at the end of both the outer axes – so at the top left of the page and the bottom right.

Well done! You just drew a 'Boston Matrix' or a 2 x 2 diagram. In my experience, doing one of these make you look like a genius.

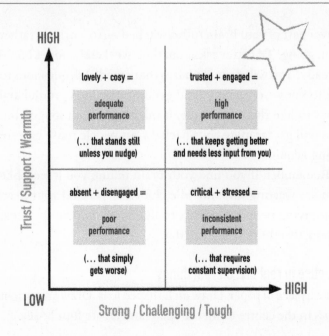

You can draw these four boxes quickly and use them in a practical way to think about what high trust and low challenge sounds like when it comes out of your mouth. Or what low trust and high challenge looks like when you move around your workplace. It can be easier to envisage what high trust *and* high challenge looks like, when you have identified what it *doesn't* look like first. I don't usually bother with the bottom left box … generally the activity in that box is to do absolutely nothing!

For an example – think about a conversation you need to have with someone. Let's call her Clare. Maybe Clare's performance has dropped off a cliff. She has delivered a report to you late. It's not the first time. Her lateness causes you to look inefficient. Think about the first lines that you could use to open this conversation and put practical examples of these words in each of the four boxes so that you can practise. You will start to see which style might be easiest for you, and where you might need to dial up either the challenge or the support.

An introduction that would 'fit' the top-left box would be high on warmth, but low on challenge. Perhaps something like:

> 'Are you OK, Clare? If you don't mind, I'd really like it if we could talk about your performance. I'm worried about you.'

Then think about the bottom-right box. This would be an introduction that is very challenging and low on warmth:

> 'What the hell is going on with you? I have had enough of you letting me down. I'm not going to tell you about your report being late again. If you don't sort it, I will.'

Then think about the top-right box. High support and high challenge. What would that introduction sound like? Try to find words that you actually use:

> 'Clare, we really need to have an open and honest conversation about what is behind your reports being late. What is not negotiable is that I absolutely have it on time from now on. I'm hoping now I have made

> that clear that you can trust me enough to talk to
> me about what is really going on here so I can
> help you work through it.'

You can use this exercise with your teams or yourself to think about almost anything. I have used it with very different audiences, from call-centre employees to help them to deal with difficult customers to executives preparing 'state-of-the-nation' style speeches.

Be top right – with or without permission

Many of the clients I work with end up deciding that a top-right leadership style is the way to go. In some cases this has led to an organisation using 'top-right leadership' as a simple framework and I have coached their whole senior team and trained their line managers to use it daily.

However, one of the great things about deciding to be more 'top right' as an individual is that it doesn't actually require any organisational infrastructure. You can decide to make your conversations and challenges belong to that top-right box tomorrow. You might not always get the balance between support and challenge, warmth and strength or approachability and authority spot on. But, with practice, you will absolutely see the difference in the power of your conversations. It's because the science is on your side.

TOP RIGHT QUESTIONS

For you

➢ When I dealt with that situation today was I more concerned to assert my authority or to build the relationship?

➢ Which quadrant did that conversation belong to?

➢ What would I do if I were going to have a 'bottom-left' approach to this situation? What about a 'bottom-right approach'? And what would 'top-left' look like? So what's 'top right' in this situation?

➢ Do I feel it is better to be liked or to be respected? What would mean I could have both?

➢ Which relationships do I have where there isn't a high level of trust right now? What could I do about that?

➢ Are there some people who I avoid challenging? What could I do to make it more likely that I would challenge them when it is required?

For others

➢ Would this situation be better if you dialled your challenge up, or provided more support or both?

➢ If I told you that my instincts suggest you could have been a little more supportive/challenging, would there be a grain of truth in that?

➢ What are your fears about being too supportive/challenging? Are those fears genuine and what evidence do you have?

➢ What will be the consequence for you if you avoid having a challenging conversation?

➢ What are the benefits or potential opportunities of building a more trusting relationship?

LEARN MORE AND SHARE

Really great read

Compelling People by John Neffinger and Matthew Kohut

An easy to read introduction to the principles of being top right. The authors draw on Amy Cuddy's research and the references are helpfully written so that you can know a little more about another book or paper before you go to the trouble of reading it.

The Five Disfunctions of a Team by Patrick Lencioni

A New York Times Best Seller with practical ideas and a simple theoretical model. His research shows how trust is the bottom building block of the team functionality "pyramid" (a bit like Maslow's hierarchy if you are familiar with it) He argues without trust, you can't build a successful team. It is widely used in sport as well as business and good for cutting through politics.

Blogs

A summary of the research in this chapter and ideal for sharing the key elements of the science:

www.itsnotbloodyrocketscience.com/uncategorized/
great-leadership-simple-to-define-really-hard-to-do/
http://zengerfolkman.com/great-leaders-move-fast/

Articles

A summary of the key principles of the *Compelling People* book can be found in Amy Cuddy, Matthew Kohut and John Neffinger, 'Connect, Then Lead', *Harvard Business Review*, July–August 2013.

A quick summary of the importance of being both liked and respected can be found here:

www.forbes.com/sites/joefolkman/2013/7/25/
exceptional-leaders-are-they-the-friend-or-the-
enemy

Internet resources

Find Deborah Gruenfeld's video *Power and Influence* on YouTube.

PARTING SHOT

High support; high challenge.

At the same time. Pretty straightforward to describe. Really hard to do. However, in my experience, clients who persist in trying to do both at the same time get results that genuinely amaze them. Results they can quantify in cash. And they confirm that it absolutely frees up some of the time they used to spend 'managing', giving them space to do some of the things they would have done but 'didn't have the time'.

That promise of more time has got to be worth challenging the cognitive miser in you, hasn't it? What one thing could you do right now to try this approach today and tomorrow? Do it. Provide your miserly brain with some good 'evidence' that it is worth the effort.

I promise. You won't be disappointed.

COACHING

Coaching, mentoring, leading and
managing – what works where and when?

THE REALLY BIG IDEA

I'm often asked to work with organisations to identify what
leadership behaviours or management skills they should
focus on to deliver increased revenues and better performance from their people.

You can spend a lot of time and money via world-class con-
sultancies that promise to help you answer this question. The
problem with that investment is that deciding that a behaviour or skill is important, and defining what 'good' looks like,
doesn't make it suddenly appear in the organisation.

In fact, if the leaders in an organisation are not doing 'the
things on the list' already, because they are human beings

with the same brain wiring we all have, those leaders who have invited me to consult are likely to:

1. Resist the list and argue for particular skills or behaviours to be left out because you can lead successfully without them. (See Chapter 1 on why our brains lie to us. Remember self-serving bias from that chapter? This is it!)

2. Think they are good at the identified skill or behaviour already (based on 'evidence') and talk about the importance of those qualities – without actually demonstrating them in daily life.

3. Commit to find the time for themselves and their teams to be trained on the skills and behaviours, but find they have too many time-pressured activities to make the training change anything on the shop or office floor.

4. Continue to model behaviours and skills that weren't on the list because 'they work'.

It is normal and natural for people to model what they see the most powerful leaders in an organisation *actually* doing, rather than what the competency paperwork details. In most organisations I have worked or consulted in the behaviours an organisation grows are those that the leaders exhibit on a daily basis. This applies equally to desirable behaviours and unfortunately to the less desirable ones. This explains why many consultancy projects with brilliant recommendations to develop particular behaviours and skills can end up gathering dust on a shelf. This applies even if those recommendations were absolutely right.

My current approach is to advise clients to save the research cash and spend their effort and resources on *actually* increasing people's skills and behaviours in just one area and to start at the top. This is because the most convincing research and neuroscience I have read all comes to the same conclusion:

The single thing you can do to improve business performance the most is learn to be a good coach.

Let's first go directly to the research. I love sharing this particular study to help executives understand that coaching isn't soft, fluffy chit-chat used when someone is struggling or upset. It is a hard-to-learn, hard-to-master, hard-edged tool in your kitbag that is essential to produce the best business results in a knowledge economy.

In 2002 Google took a bold step. They decided to do away with managers altogether. They had highly motivated people who seemed willing and able to be accountable for themselves, so it wasn't clear to the executives at Google what the 'point' of management was. The experiment didn't work and a management layer was added back in, but it led to some fascinating research being created about how managers add value and what they should spend time doing. Google helped to define what managers are for. The study is exceptional because it illustrated scientifically that when you take something away altogether, it becomes clear what its contribution was – a bit like a zero based budgetting exercise for management qualities!

The investigation was undertaken using rigorous research and data principles. Google apply the same high bar that they have for their business operation to their HR processes when it comes to identifying talent and deciding how to train their leaders. As a result, their research into 'why managers matter' was empirical, had high validity and was carried out by PhD-level researchers who deliberately stayed as bias-free as possible. This has led me to accept their findings more easily than I have in the past when other organisations (with a commercial interest in selling me a leadership-behaviour model) have told me what the top ten qualities are in a good manager.

Google looked from the bottom up. By first looking at what happens without a manager, they tested the generally held contention that 'management' of some sort is necessary to ensure that people are organised and held to account to deliver results. They were then able to examine which different behaviours most closely correlated to improved business performance when they put those managerial 'tasks' back in.

Google were able to create a definitive list of the things that managers do that definitely improve business performance and make managers worth having. Given that Google have a waiting list of employees who want to work for them, I'm going to agree with their findings until someone with an equally successful business comes up with something empirically better.

So, drumroll please …

The top three behaviours or skills identified by Google as essential for managers to possess are:

1. Be a good coach.

2. Empower the team and don't micromanage.

3. Expresses interest in and concern for team-member success and personal wellbeing.

Being results oriented, having a good technical skills and having a clear vision and strategy made the top ten, but far and away the biggest indicator of superior performance in engineers in Google was having a manager who was a good coach. It was number 1 by quite some margin.

Thus, when I am developing a programme for leaders and managers, it always contains an element of coaching skill because that skill is where Google found the biggest bang for their managerial buck. I might also cover creating a powerful vision or giving challenging feedback, but I tend to use coaching skill as a platform to do these other things.

The concept that coaching should be a business priority for senior leaders rather than a 'nice to do' for some of the HR team isn't rocket science or even especially new thinking. As a result, it is not difficult to convince clients that coaching training will add value. However, one of the biggest barriers to learning to be a good coach is highlighted in point 2 on the previous page: we think we are good at it already. When I recommend coaching as part of a training programme, many leaders or managers will tell me that they coach all the time;

that coaching skills might be a bit basic for the audience and that we can probably cover it quite quickly.

I include myself in this. Most of the research I refer to wasn't around when I was developing my managerial behaviours and skills. I and other leaders in the Generation X or Baby Boomer years developed our management 'habits' and became successful without knowing what coaching was or the brain science about why it works. When I started to hear that good coaching involved asking challenging questions whilst being supportive, it was easy to think, 'Great! That sounds like what I do already.'

It was only when I went to Henley Business School to learn to become a professional coach that I realised I actually wasn't a good coach at all. I had some skills that I had labelled 'coaching' – such as taking time when training people and asking people questions like the '5 Whys' to help them overcome resistance. I was doing this with positive intent and I thought I was well informed about good questions to ask people. For example in the case of asking 'Why?' five times, I had been reliably informed that this was a good problem-solving technique that originated in root-cause analysis and had been used by Toyota in the 1980s. I had thought these questioning techniques were working well for me, but the more I got to know, the more I realised that these sorts of questions were not coaching and were actually quite the opposite. For example, asking 'Why?' a lot, might well be good for root-cause analysis, but using the word 'why', I found out was the antithesis of coaching, because it sometimes caused people to be defensive and blocked their thinking. In short, I thought I had productive 'coaching' habits already, but I learnt that I hadn't. Indeed, persisting with them was preventing me from getting the business benefits that coaching properly can deliver.

In my experience of teaching people to coach over the past ten years, I have come to know I'm not alone. Many of the behaviours and skills that my clients have developed and labelled 'coaching' are absolutely not coaching. Don't get me wrong, those skills and behaviours are not necessarily bad human qualities. They are well intentioned and sometimes helpful things that we all say and do – such as making suggestions ('This what I'd do if I were you') or sympathising ('Gosh, I totally understand, I'm feeling the pressure too') or helping people avoid mistakes by directing ('I think this might work better than what you are suggesting').

The word 'coaching' has lots of other connotations and means different things to different people however. The coaching skills that increase business performance are very specific. Coaching, in this context and put simply, is about helping people's brains to think better. It is about increasing brain power.

What feedback has taught me is that I am good at helping people to understand how to do things. But this is not coaching. It is teaching and training. Training provides useful information or relevant skills but does not of itself increase our ability to think better.

Some things that we label "coaching" are good things to do. But absolutely aren't coaching.

I'm happy to share my experience (and many failures) with others in a mentoring capacity and I am often asked to give advice and support. But whilst giving advice and sharing your experiences is helpful, it is not coaching. Giving advice does not increase the brain power of the recipient.

I'm incessantly curious and able to construct clever questions (and am brave enough to ask them), but I know in the past that I wasn't using those questions to coach. More often, I was using my clever questions to win the argument or bring people round to my way of thinking. In my defence I usually believed I was doing something positive and that my way of thinking would help someone. But asking questions to lead people to your conclusion does not help other people to think better for themselves. It is therefore not coaching. It is something else.

The things not to do when you are coaching are important to understand – not because you will get into trouble with any corporate body for getting it wrong, but because those 'don't do's' can create impulses in the brain that are so powerful that they shut down our ability to think. They can undermine our efforts to use coaching to get someone to think better.

People I train often tell me they don't have time to coach. They are partly right. You probably don't have time to start coaching but then stop listening properly and as a result fall into telling people what to do partway through. Starting to coach but not finishing as a coach is a waste of time. You won't get the business benefits that come with helping them think better for themselves. And it took longer than just telling someone what to do in the first place.

Semantics aside, because 'coaching' has become a by-word

for good management and leadership, it is to be expected that many of us will describe ourselves as having a 'coaching approach' or having 'coaching conversations' – even if we don't. The last thing our brains want is to feel exposed. Our brains would find it very difficult to acknowledge that something is important but that we don't know how to we try but fail and slip into giving advise instead. I want to reassure you that *not* remembering to coach is not surprising. Your own very human brain is likely to find coaching difficult. Coaching involves untangling some of those 'lies' from Chapter 1 and thinking about the evidence of our own eyes differently, which we discussed in Chapters 2 and 3.

We know from these chapters that it is really difficult to untangle your truth from your lies without feedback or difficult reflection. As a result the real benefits of coaching are likely to take some time to come through because they rely on people doing something new and uncomfortable that their brains will argue takes up too much energy and therefore is a waste of time. You almost need a coach to be a coach. Someone to help you to retrain your brain so that you can help others to do the same.

It is hard to accept as a manager that things you are doing with positive intent such as making suggestions, sympathising and directing your staff – that you will probably remove an opportunity for someone to learn to think differently.

Of course, there is an upside to not coaching: if your people don't learn to think better for themselves, they will always need your help and you will probably always be in a job and visibly working hard!

The reason that this chapter comes directly after Top Right is that the two chapters are strongly connected. When I am training people to coach, the first thing I help people to understand is that being a good coach requires you to be warm and strong at the same time. To make people feel challenged AND supported. If you don't have both, you can't coach. Coaching simply doesn't work if you don't do both things together because our brains don't respond well to excessive challenge/coercion or being told what to do.

Chapter 5 explained the SCARF reaction. This helps us to understand what happens when we 'over-challenge'. Recall Google's second most important management activity: don't micromanage. I don't want to repeat what is covered elsewhere, so by way of a super-quick summary:

➤ Our brains don't respond well to being told what to do or what someone else thinks is best.

➤ Our brains don't respond well when people we don't like challenge us.

➤ People don't perform at their best when they are being micromanaged.

➤ People perform best with ongoing, informal, stretching feedback from someone they trust.

That's why coaching works for us as human beings – it covers those very bases and creates a positive cycle:

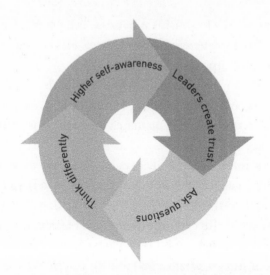

➤ Leaders and managers who coach create a high-trust environment where challenging questions and feedback are the norm.

➤ Rather than telling them what to do, coaching leaders ask questions of their people that challenge their assumptions about their work, behaviours, talents and motivations.

➤ These questions force their people to use their brains differently resulting in their people learning to think in more effective ways.

➤ The end result is higher self-awareness leading to better decisions, less task avoidance, higher emotional intelligence and increased trust.

Coaching works for business because it helps your people perform better when you are not there. Hence you can get on with something else. Win–win.

The problem is that even after you understand what coaching is, and that it requires warmth and strength being deployed *together*, combining these two qualities is pretty difficult to do.

What is more usual in my experience is that we start out intending to coach that way, but then we revert to telling people what to think. We tell ourselves we don't have time, or that coaching isn't appropriate for that particular scenario. Chapter 1 on the lies our brains tell us should help you understand your own resistance and to help you to explore these common excuses about time or situational applicability.

In the meantime, if you want to prove to yourself today that giving advice and suggestions doesn't work as well as you thought it did, here's something you can try.

In his fabulous book *Quiet Leadership*, David Rock challenges you to keep a note of every piece of advice you are given in a week. To review that advice and see which bits of it you took on board at the end of the week. My bet (and, I'm guessing, his) is that you get a lot of advice and you listen to very little of it. Try it for just one day. Personally, I didn't need to repeat it for seven.

GOT IT – NOW WHAT?

Not coaching? don't worry: knowing that is a good start

If you read this chapter and realise that when you describe yourself as 'coaching' you are actually more accurately supporting, teaching, mentoring, managing (or dare I say manipulating?), then good. You are now officially consciously incompetent. Anyone who works in learning will tell you that recognising that you aren't naturally good at something is the first step to learning it and becoming competent. My experience of working with many managers and leaders in lots of organisations would also put you in some very good and successful company if you feel this way. I hope the simple tips on how to start to coach 'properly' as well as doing those other things, could start to save you time, elevate the performance of your teams and make you more money quickly.

Be clear and honest with yourself about what coaching is and what it is not

When I am training people to coach I usually get three or four groups to brainstorm what the similarities and differences are between:

➢ coaching and mentoring

➢ coaching and training

➢ coaching and managing

➢ business coaching and sports coaching.

You can use this activity to create two columns of words or activities. In the first column you list the things that apply to both coaching and mentoring/training etc. such as 'listening skills' and 'having a goal'. In the second column you list things that don't apply to coaching, but that are good skills for a when you are mentoring or training – such as 'Being explicit about how to do something' or 'Saying no'.

COACHING

- Listening and Asking Questions
- Conversation where the goal is flexible and the options are open
- They have the expertise – you unlock it
- They are learning for themselves
- Asking questions to help people think about what they could do
- Allowing silence and space for them to think
- Offering a safe place to be honest
- Being non-judgemental and holding back on making assumptions

GOOD THINGS WE DO – THAT AREN'T COACHING

- Giving Advice and offering support
- Conversation without a shared goal or where options are fixed
- You have the expertise – you share it
- They are learning from you
- Showing someone what to do
- Suggesting what someone could do
- Filling awkward silences
- Offering Reassurance
- Making sensible judgements, assumptions and assessments

I have found that it helps to list the things that are coaching and those that are not coaching. It means that when you are learning to coach, you can reflect on how well you stick to doing the things in the first column and how well you studiously avoid the things in the second column.

Reflect — be honest with yourself about your motives for choosing NOT to coach

Most of the items in your right-hand column above, such as making suggestions, sympathising, directing (and being quite blunt) are things I still do. They remain part of my managerial toolkit. The difference is that I now use those tools deliberately to get a particular job done, knowing full well that they are absolutely *not* coaching. In fact they can actively suppress some of the benefits of coaching, so I keep in mind that whatever tool I'm using for the job has particular consequences. I'm honest with myself when I am reflecting (remember Chapter 7) about whether I might need to revisit a conversation because I didn't do it justice the first time round. For example, if I genuinely only have time to give advice when there is a really good coaching opportunity that would save time in the long run, I don't beat myself for not having time, I make a mental note to go back and have the conversation that would add value.

Giving a quick bit of advice when you know you should ask questions and coach is a bit like hanging a picture: you want up and out of the way. You haven't the time to get the drill and the spirit level out, so you whack an old nail in the wall to get the job done. The picture is up. It stays up.

The problem comes when you start to worry when someone sits under the picture at your next dinner party. Or when you regularly promise yourself that you will hang it properly when you have time. It's on your mind. It's taking up space and thus energy. The quick fix hasn't actually solved the problem, it's merely postponed it. You know there was a better tool for the job, and that your old nail hasn't given you the same result that using the right tools would have.

If you replace an opportunity to coach with a quick fix but find the 'picture' is still wonky or it's still on your mind, that's normal. My advice is to ask yourself one of my favourite reflective questions:

'What better question I could have asked?'

Then go and find the time to ask it.

Ignore almost all of the coaching models

At Henley Business School I was taught that you learn a lot of models to forget most of them. The one I come back to, and the most simple model in my view, is known as GROW. I was lucky enough to connect with its creator, Sir John Whitmore, shortly before he died. GROW gives a very simple sequential problem-solving structure where we ask questions and listen in order to:

G – Establish the GOAL of the conversation
R – Enable **them** to understand the REALITY of what is going on
O – Enable **them** to create OPTIONS for themselves
W – Enable **them** to decide WHAT NOW? What do they have the WILL to do about it?

The word ***them*** is in bold italics for a reason. This is not about *you* understanding what is going on and deciding what next steps they should take. Or using your experience. Remember, coaching works because you are helping people to think better for *themselves*.

We are most likely to follow through with the ideas that *we* came up with. We are very good at avoiding things we have been *ordered* to do. We are very disinclined to *disregard* the advice we are given.

Still think coaching is a nice-to-have, 'fluffy' HR type of thing?

What? Even though Google think it is the Number 1 thing that all managers should do? OK. Here's an example of one of the least-fluffy organisations in the world using it. The US Army developed something in the 1990s that looks pretty much like coaching – they just called it something different – an After Action Review, or AAR. The AAR is a structured review or debrief process that helps to analyse what happened, why it happened and how things could be done better next time. You can use the principles of an AAR at work if you are worried about using the word 'coaching'. Have a go at asking these questions whilst everything is fresh in people's minds:

➢ What was supposed to happen?

➢ What did happen?

➢ What can be done better next time?

➤ What should we keep doing because it worked?

➤ Who's going to do what to make sure this happens?

'I don't have the time to coach'

A formal executive coaching session usually lasts about ninety minutes. So you might be right that, if you have ten direct reports, fitting in ninety minutes of coaching for each of them every week is going to be difficult. But who says you have to? Coaching is something you can do in the moment. Coaching questions are something you can introduce into your existing conversations.

I help people to understand that there are three occasions (broadly speaking) when you can have a coaching conversation. They can be

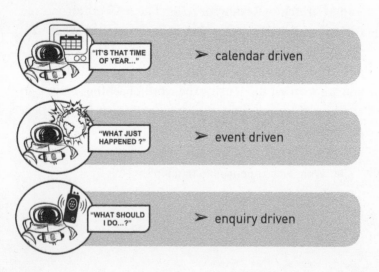

➤ calendar driven

➤ event driven

➤ enquiry driven

Calendar-driven coaching happens during a prearranged coaching meeting or performance improvement conversation that you both know is going to happen and can prepare for. It might be annual, but it is better if the session is monthly, fortnightly or weekly.

You might even get ahead of the curve. In a recent study, 77 per cent of HR executives reported that their top priority is encouraging more-frequent performance management conversations (i.e. weekly or monthly, as opposed to 'annual performance reviews'). So having shorter, sharper and more focused conversations based on coaching principles every week or month might eventually replace the dreaded APR that everyone hates, managers and employees alike. Surely it is worth giving it a go for that reason alone?

Event-driven coaching resembles the US Army's AAR: something happens and you then get together to discuss it and use a coaching approach to find out what went right and wrong so that you can learn from it.

Enquiry-driven coaching is coaching in the moment. Someone asks you 'What should I do about this?' Rather than answering it with, 'Well what I would do is ...' You ask a coaching question instead. Try, 'What do *you* think the options are?' It's a handy response to most things that you can easily keep up your sleeve.

To be a good coach, you might have to give some things up

In my pre-coaching life, I prided myself on being the fountain of all knowledge in the jobs I did. Knowing everything about everything – whether that be employment law or how to increase spend per head in a restaurant. I loved being able to solve people's problems for them by drawing on that bank of knowledge and telling them, with confidence, what to do.

I was really busy as a 'go-to' girl. Too busy, in fact. As I became a coach, I also realised there was a potential flaw in what I was doing, psychologically speaking. In telling people what to do based on my own experience, I wasn't helping them to think about what they could do based on their own insights. I was training them to come to me for everything. And they did – hence why I was so 'in demand' and busy. That felt good. I had evidence that I was 'useful'. People said thank you. I felt appreciated. Repeat.

However, I was not doing the thing I needed to do most – helping people to think for themselves.

Sometimes the most difficult feedback to hear is what helps us the most

The feedback that has been the most influential in my life probably hurt the most to receive. When we receive critical feedback about something that we are doing with really positive intent, it can be difficult to hear, but it's important that you try really hard to use it.

In my case, this happened when someone I trusted pointed out something fundamental about my management style and my 'coaching': *Dulcie, you are stealing the opportunity for other people to learn.*

Helping people is in my DNA. I love it. I go out of my way to give someone a hand. So initially, I resisted. I explained the feedback away, but I physically and mentally forced myself to start an experiment. When someone came to ask me a question and I had a view on it, rather than answer straightaway with, 'Well what I would do is ...', I did something different.

I waited for a moment before speaking.

It can be so hard to do this type of experiment – particularly when your professional experience and success is based to some extent on the very thing that you are trying to *stop* doing. I was so proud of being able to quickly pull an answer out of the hat for almost any situation in Operations, HR or Organisational Change that I would never pause to reflect. With coaching training and that 'steal' feedback firmly locked in my brain, I now always pause. And subconsciously I repeat to myself the second most valuable but difficult piece of feedback I received around that time: *Dulcie, it is never too late to make an intervention. But in your case it can often be too early.*

I have now trained myself change my mindset during that brief pause between thinking I will say something and it actually coming out of my mouth. Scientists reckon the pause is 0.2 seconds, so it is quite hard work, but I use the split-second pause to put my brain into 'curious' mode rather than 'fix it' mode. I then ask myself about the question I have just heard.

Is the questioner asking for a clear yes or no or for my

personal opinion or for my specific feedback? Having decided which, I answer the question based on my knowledge and experience.

If I'm asked 'Is this legal?' or 'Do you think I did a good job in that presentation?' I must decide whether the person is asking me because they have a skill gap – that is to say they just don't know something – or a will gap – they lack confidence or need reassurance.

If I sense it is a skill-gap question, I seek confirmation by asking 'Is this something you have similar experience of already?'

If my instincts are that it is a will-gap question, I ask something non-judgemental that makes it safe for them to ask for affirmation or reassurance: 'I'm sensing you might be looking for me to approve of your idea, rather than for my opinion?'

When you are trying to coach, get feedback. Work on the pieces of feedback that hurt the most. The things you find most difficult. The things your brain really wants to resist and explain away. I bet that's where your dynamite is.

'Nobody coaches in my organisation — it's not one of our "leadership behaviours"'

When I am recommending *A Mind of Its Own* by Cordelia Fine I ask people to look at her biography. Her first degree is from Oxford, her Masters is from Cambridge, her research PhD is from Harvard and she now tutors at Melbourne University. In short, even if you are uncomfortable with some of the messages from her books, she probably knows much better than you or I about the science of human behaviour. She talks in a very straightforward way about the self-serving bias we met in Chapter 1. In a nutshell, we give greater credibility to leadership behaviours that we ourselves possess – that have worked for us. Our brains lead us to believe that if we have managed without a certain skill or behaviour then it is not likely to be that important and is something that can be worked around.

When organisations are defining leadership behaviours or management-selection criteria, they need to be very careful to avoid biased towards the existing behaviours of the people who are compiling the list. This means that if your current leaders don't coach, they are not likely to believe that coaching will be as effective as the methods they use to get results.

So if there is a leadership behaviour that would make a real difference to the organisation, even if it is trained in, it won't become part of the culture if the CEO does the opposite. People might agree that developing a skill or behaviour (such as coaching) is a good idea, but they won't actually focus on developing it away from the classroom.

The great thing is, though, that you can try some of the things in this chapter without anyone's permission or any corporate infrastructure. The organisation doesn't need to decide that everyone is going to try coaching for you to try it first.

If you want a coach, find a good one

Not every director or CEO makes a good coach. At Henley I was surrounded by directors of big businesses – FTSE 100 companies that are household names. These were successful leaders with six-figure salaries who had come to learn to coach. You might ask who am I to judge, but I'm going to anyway. I would estimate that at the end of the twelve-month programme, 20 per cent of them had become really great coaches. I discerned a trend whereby people who had succeeded in business without being good coaches found coaching really hard to do.

Some of the people I met were really impressive. They had an answer for everything and seemed invincible; they had 'been there and done that' and were happy to share their advice and give you a view on your issue. I am sure they were great mentors and probably good leaders, but many of them were not great at coaching.

What I noticed about myself and about the coaching I observed (we monitored each other to provide feedback) was that the coachee was much more likely to be honest and reflec-tive with coaches who didn't talk much about themselves. It was the people without 'ego' – those who focused entirely on me and not on what they could do to 'help' – who were actu-ally much more helpful. There is nothing wrong with wanting to help people, but helping them by telling them what you would do is not coaching. It's direction. It seemed to me that many of the people who had retired from the boardroom at the very top of their game and now wanted to coach actually wanted to share what they had done and how they had done it. It made for fascinating listening, but not for fantastic coaching.

There's no time like the present

I'm assuming you have read this far because you agree that coaching matters and it is something you want to learn to do.

There are a million definitions of what coaching is, so I won't add another. My advice is give it a go right now. Try coaching one of your team during a telephone call to that you were going to make today anyway (that way you can keep these notes in front of you.). It works best if you need to have a slightly tricky conversation about something they are avoiding, haven't done or you need feedback about.

Here's the plan:

Get yourself into a 'top right' frame of mind (see Chapter 9). If you can't, or don't like the person or are convinced they are beyond redemption, don't bother trying to coach them – it won't work. Try another time with someone else.

Write the letters G R O W down the left hand side of a piece of paper. You are going to use the GROW model we met on page 230 to have a sequential conversation with someone.

By the side of the G, state your GOAL for the conversation. Write down your opening line. Be clear on what you want to get out of the discussion. Take a bit of time to get this first line right; make sure the language you are going to use is as authentic and as 'top right' as you can get it. You are looking for a tone which is warm and supportive to deliver a statement or question which is tough and challenging.

Let's assume someone has not done something you asked them to do, and that this has happened before. You are going to think about what a bottom-left, top-left, bottom-right and top-right introductory sentence or two might be so you can practise them first.

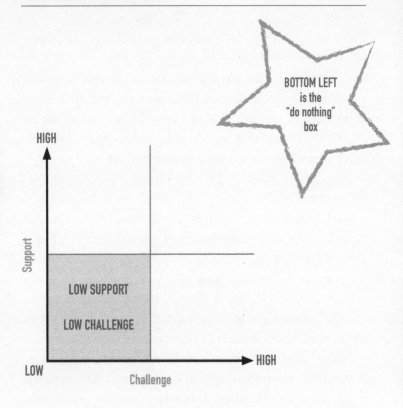

Bottom left: This would be an approach where you decide to do nothing and resolve to see what happens next time instead. You provide no support and no challenge.

I hardly ever recommend this approach. In my experience you just get a longer period of average performance and you still have to have the challenging conversation a week/month/year.

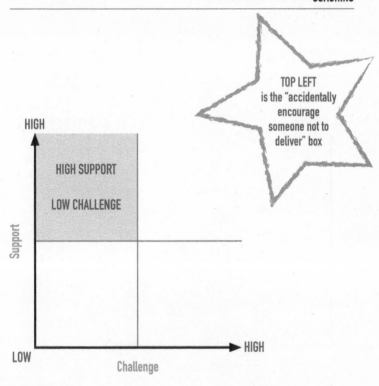

Top left: A top-left way of introducing the conversation might go: 'Hi, Bob ... sorry to interrupt what you were doing, I'm sure you are busy but I wanted to see where you are up to with the report I asked for? It might be I haven't seen it and you have sent it ... blah blah blah.' If this is the way you would introduce a difficult conversation, then rework it. It's too long. Don't apologise. Don't belittle the importance of what you asking someone to do. It makes it more likely they won't see it as a priority.

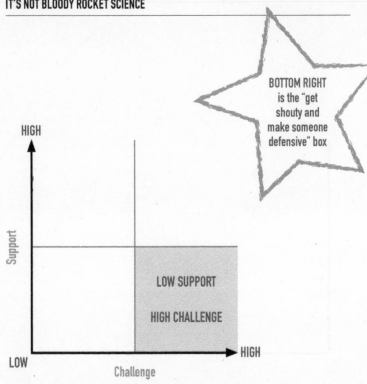

BOTTOM RIGHT is the "get shouty and make someone defensive" box

HIGH

Support

LOW SUPPORT

HIGH CHALLENGE

LOW

HIGH

Challenge

Bottom right: A bottom-right way of introducing the conversation might go: 'It's me. Why haven't I had the report yet? It's not good enough.' Mmmm. You didn't even say 'Hi'?

Bob's defences are probably already up (maybe you have created the SCARF reaction in him and for the rest of the conversation his brain is operating at 20 per cent thinking capacity). Using 'Why' means his brain will get defensive for sure. He'll probably lie, make excuses or apologise profusely and say you will get the report later, but you will be none the wiser about why this keeps happening and have to repeat this conversation next week.

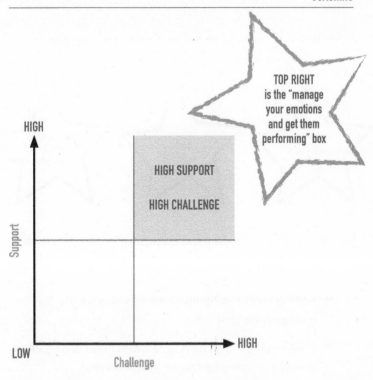

Top right: Finally, a top-right introduction might go: 'Hi, Bob. Listen, I need us to have an open and honest conversation about what the real reasons are that your report is late again so that we can fix the problem for good. I've got time to talk now, so that we don't put off getting to the heart of the issue. Is now good for you?'

Practise saying this out loud a couple of times so it sound natural rather than scripted. You might feel like a fool but I promise it works.

Remember, when you coach as a manager, you are doing nothing more and nothing less than:

Stating your position in a top-right way

Asking questions

Listening without prejudice

In my experience the hardest things for people to practise are:

➤ putting their own opinions aside and resisting giving advice, and

➤ resisting the temptation to respond immediately or to disagree with, correct or advise them.

To stop yourself doing these things:

➤ Pause to think about what the person you are speaking to has just said (and what your instinct says they are not telling you).

➤ When you ask a question, listen very carefully to what that person says in return.

➢ When you want to offer an idea, advice or an
  opinion, ask another question instead
  (e.g. replace 'If I were you I would ...' with 'What
  are the options as you see it?')

➢ Avoid using the word 'why' and use the word 'what'
  (e.g. replace 'Why did you do that?' with 'What
  made you feel that was the right call at the time?')

If you are stuck for a question, either:

➢ Say nothing and let them fill the awkward silence.
  If they ask if you are still there you can say,
  'Yes, I'm listening.'

➢ Take a word that they have just used and turn it
  into a question
  (e.g. Them: 'I'm worried about this report.' You:
  'Worried?')

➢ Repeat a word or phrase they have used and add
  'Tell me more about that.'
  (e.g. 'You said you felt "under the cosh" – tell me
  more about that.')

When you are new to coaching I suggest you use the GROW
model to have a sequential conversation to solve a problems
logically. This matches what the human brain does when it
problem solves. The sequence is easy to follow:

Use GOAL questions to establish what you are going to talk about.

Then explore the REALITY of what is going on. Ask the person questions to create OPTIONS.

Talk to them about which of those options they WILL actually do.

You can find a wide variety of questions at TopRightQuestions.com. Try these to start with.

To clarify the GOAL

➤ 'What would good look like at the end of this fifteen-minute conversation?'

➤ 'What specifically are you trying to achieve?'

To explore the REALITY

➤ 'What do you think is really going on?'

➤ 'Could you share with me what you think is at the heart of the problem?'

To create OPTIONS

➤ 'So what options do you have?'

➤ 'What else could you do?'

To test their WILL and get a WHAT NEXT

> 'What will you actually commit to doing?'

> 'What might stop you?'

> 'How could I help to make sure it happens?'

Give it a go and see what happens. Most people who are learning to coach report that:

> It was extremely difficult not to give an opinion or offer help.

> They were able to cover a surprisingly large amount of ground in a relatively short conversation.

> They'd like to know more about coaching because it seemed to work.

TOP RIGHT QUESTIONS

In addition to the Top Right Questions below and in this chapter, I also run a blog – TopRightQuestions.com where I encourage people to share their best questions. Here are two simple and fast GROW sequences that work almost anytime and anywhere!

For you

➤ If I am really honest with myself, what is the real goal I want to achieve?

➤ What is really going on that I am trying hard to avoid?

➤ What could I do right now that would do no harm and might make a difference?

➤ What will I do this minute before I talk myself out of it?

For others

➤ How would you describe what you want to get from this conversation in one sentence?

➤ What do your instincts tell you is at the heart/core of the problem?

➤ What 3 things could you do that might help?

➤ Is there a difference between what you could do and what you know you will actually do?

LEARN MORE AND SHARE

Really great read

The Coaches Coach by Alison Hardingham with Mike Brearley, Adrian Moorhouse, and Brendan Venter
An excellent book co-written by three ex-sportsmen turned coaches, so there are lots of practical and interesting stories as well.

GROW Coach for Performance by Sir John Whitmore
Easy to read with lots of tips on how to use GROW with individuals and teams.

Blog

This blog has some suggestions about how to use the GROW model for different things. It can be used by managers to embed learning from training programmes that their team attend or to have difficult performance conversations

https://changeyourmindfast.com/2016/02/12/
different-ways-to-use-grow/

Article

The research at Google where they removed managers in order to identify what day to day activities were of real importance to the business is widely commented on and available by simply typing the three words HBR Google Management into a search engine. Or find it at:.

https://hbr.org/2013/12/how-google-sold-its-engineers-on-management/

Internet resources

I have set up a website called Top Right Questions where coaches can share their favourite and best questions. There are some great ones on there and a fuller list of questions that you can use at the G R O and W stages of your conversations.

https://toprightquestions.com/about/

PARTING SHOT

Coaching works because it challenges the 'miserly' human brain (that doesn't want to expend energy on thinking) to think. Google thinks coaching is the most important thing that managers need to learn to do. They are probably right. It makes sense that, in a knowledge economy, improving the brains of the people who work for us is the most important thing we can do.

Recognising the importance of coaching, doesn't mean it's easy to implement – mostly because learning to coach requires us to challenge our own miserly brain ... But if it was easy, everyone would be doing it already.

And it not being easy? Well, that doesn't make it impossible, does it?

FINAL, FINAL WORD

We've covered a lot of ground and referenced thousands of pages of work by real experts in their field. However, none of them is an expert on *you*. That's why the hard work happens when you put these words into practice. It's only then when you try and sometimes succeed and try and sometimes fail that you will find out what particular brain tricks *your* mind might play in order to keep you doing exactly what *you* have always done.

Remind yourself that, as you try and fail, your normal human brain is wired to:

1. Tell you **lies** about what you can achieve

2. Get really tired and distracted and tell you that **working harder** is the only answer

3. **Disregard evidence** and get fact-brain freeze

4. Make you feel like an **Imposter**

5. Cause you to threaten some people by accident or feel the **SCARF** reaction yourself

6. Try to convince you that the world would be better if everyone was just a **bit more like you**

7. Agree it's **good to reflect**, but find good reasons to dwell on things you can't change instead

8. Convince you *not* **to change** – and even to lay down and die instead

9. Tell you that being **supportive and challenging** are not qualities you can display together

10. Tell you **coaching** is fluffy HR rubbish and that you are better off micro-managing everyone

Back to the quote that started us off: 'Only a fool or a liar would say that they understand the human brain'. Recent science is only just starting to help us to understand ourselves. Most of us will be retired before the science is even nearly conclusive.

We have to start somewhere. Helpfully for my own brain, I realised that I needed to give up hope of writing a perfect book about brain science as it would never get finished!

Instead I hope simply to have brought some of the breakthroughs from scientists and academic researchers to ordinary people living everyday lives in the real world. I hope, if you have got this far, that you appreciate you don't need to read all that much in order to do quite a lot.

So, get a cup of tea and have a quick look at Chapter 1 again – maybe just the Parting Shot to remind you of what you already know. Try some of the suggestions when the tea break is over. If it helps, have another cuppa tomorrow and skim read Chapter 2. That's it. Imperfect but 'good enough' leadership made super simple. One cup of tea at a time.

ACKNOWLEDGEMENTS

First and foremost to my wonderful friend and the exceptionally talented business woman that is Sarah Walden. It is fair to say that without her sense of urgency, lovely way of chivvying me along and my professional respect for her (meaning I actually believed it might be true, when she said my early draft was really good), this book would never have left my PC. She has been the epitome of high support and high challenge throughout the pleasure and pain of writing this book. It simply wouldn't exist without her. Sarah, you are ace. Please never stop being my top right friend for life. I hope to sit in your new kitchen drinking expensive wine really soon!

Thanks to the many people who read chapters in blog or book form and engaged in debates with me about the science and research. You provided me with some fantastic insights, many examples of the practical ideas working in real life and great suggestions for further reading and references. The book and its ideas wouldn't have been nearly as well researched and robustly tested in real life without you. Many thanks to Jade Costello, Head of People and Tony Griffin, Operations Director for Gusto Restaurants, Sally Baker, Head of People – City Division, Helen Stuttard, Head of Retail Recruitment and Alison Bradbury, Head of People – Restaurant Division at Mitchells and Butlers, Katie White, Learning and Development Manager, MAB and MA Psychology and Neurophysiology – University of Oxford, Amanda Harvey, Head of Talent Development at Carpetright, Joanne

Mears of DPA Management Consultants, Victoria Roberts, Psychology undergraduate – Warwick University, Ken McPherson, Chief Financial Officer at the EDAM Group, Matthew Howcroft, Operations Manager, Bella Italia, Demi van der Venter, Head of People at Casual Dining Group, Maddelena Connor, General Manager at Las Iguanas, Mini Vivek, Concessions Manager at Strava, Heathrow T3, Florent Vialan Director of Brewing and Claire James, Sales Support Manager at Purity Brewing, Sarah Collett, HR and Reward Manager and Tom Arundel, Senior Product Manager at Catton Hospitality, Vanessa Greenwood and Richard Glass, Head of Operations, at Tesco Hospitality, Neil Garvin, Director at Garvins Law Limited and Wayne Morgan, Consultant People Director.

I am so sorry if in the five years this book has taken to write, I sent you a chapter and have now forgotten to thank you. The idea of not being appreciative will keep me up at night, so please send me a nice nudge if that was you and I will say thank you in hopefully the next edition (and I will owe you beer).

Thank you to Nikki Yeomans for the many debates about the science and for finally coaching me out of the PhD. I owe you several years of life.

Thank you to Mark Bennington for his fabulous illustrations throughout and for the other brilliant ways in which he has brought my science and research to life.

Thanks to Ann Childs for the absolutely wonderful cover that got my early readers excited enough to open it!

Thanks to Trevor Horwood for an amazingly thorough job of copy editing more 'so's, 'and's, 'but's and colloquial irks than you could shake a stick at.

Thanks to Dan Prescott at Couper Street for a brilliant typesetting job which gave the book exactly the mix of fun and seriousness I was after.

Thanks to Alex Swanston for the referencing, additional research into the sources and for learning to typeset for the draft version. You did a great job Alex, thank you.

Thanks to Elizabeth Davis who co-founded Tea Break Training with me and helped me to get so many of the theories and concepts that I talk about in the book turned into bite-sized training sessions to help individuals and teams to use the science. Thanks for that and everything else you have done to create the space for me to think and write Elizabeth.

Thanks to Kadisha and Oliver Lewis-Roberts who were always there to provide great suggestions for further reading and research. And more gin. Thanks to them also for introducing me to Damian Hughes – Damian, in one single conversation you made me believe that although it was difficult, writing a book was absolutely something I should do because I had something to say. Thank you.

Thanks also to Roger Steare and Paula Hall for their advice on how to turn starting to write a book into actually finishing writing a book...

Thanks to Neil Dawson for proof reading and reminding me about the "simple brain" quote after my Linked in plea!

Thanks to Laura Ashley-Timms and the team at Notion who I partnered with to introduce coaching at Mitchells and Butlers and who first introduced me to the HBR study on reflection and the 4 Ds.

With thanks to Gary Mitchell, Group HR Director, Clare Charity Group Learning and Development Manager and Steve Turner CEO of the EDAM group for giving Top Right Leadership (and thus Chapter 9) a tough work-out in real life.

With thanks to Mark Allison of Digital Opinion, who provided the most recent data for the links between engagement and profit levers.

Thanks to everyone who has donated their favourite question to TopRightQuestions.com, many of which are quoted here. Particular thanks to Lyra Cobb whose Top Right Question "How is the book going Mum?" probably had a lot to do with it getting finished.

And finally, thank you, Jamie, for physically and intellectually intimidating the blagging police so they cleared off for a bit. Without you, I'd have talked about writing a book and setting up a business all day long – but never have mustered the courage to actually do it. Love you more.

REFERENCES

ALRED.D (2016) The Pressure Principle. London: Penguin Life.

AUTRY.J (2001) The servant leader. New York: Three Rivers Press.

BLAKEY.J and DAY.I (2013) Challenging Coaching. London: Nicholas Brealey Publishing.

BJERGEGAARD.M & MILNE.J (2013) Winning Without Losing. London: Profile.

BOOTH.A & MAZUR.A (1998) Testosterone and Social Dominance in Men. National Centre for Biotechnology Information.

BOOTH.A & SHELLY.G & MAZUR.A & THARP.G (1989) TESTOSTERONE AND WINNING AND LOSING IN HUMAN COMPETITION. National Centre for Biotechnology Information

BUCKINGHAM.M (2005) the One thing you need to Know about managing great leading and sustained individual success. London: Simon & Schuster.

BURLEY-ALLEN.M (1995) Listening the forgotten skill. USA: John Wiley and Sons, Inc.

BURTON.S (2000) Imposters Six Kinds of Liar. London: Viking.

CLANCE.P.R (1995) The Imposter Phenomenon. Atlanta: Peachtree.

CLANCE.P.R & DINGMAN.D & REVIERE. S.L & STOBER. D.R Imposter phenomenon in a personal/ social context. Women and Therapy, 16, 79-96.

CLANCE.P.R & IMES.S (1978) The imposter phenomenon in high achieving women dynamic and therapeutic intervention. Psychotherapy: theory research and practise 15 241-247.

COREY.S (2004) 7 Habits of Highly Effective People. The Free Press.

COWMAN S.E & FERRARI J.R (2002) *Am I for real? Predicting imposter tendencies from self-handicapping and affectionate components.* Social behaviour and personality 30 119-125.

CUDDY.A; KOHUT.M & NEFFINGER.J (2013) *Connect, Then Lead.* Harvard Business Review

CUDDY.A & FISKE.S & GLICK.P (2007) *Universal Dimensions of Social Cognition.* Science Direct.

CUDDY.A & FISKE.S & GLICK.P (2008) *Warmth and Competence as Universal Dimensions of Social Perception: The Stereotype Content Model and the BIAS Map.* Advances in Experimental Social Psychology. New York Academic Press.

DANZIGER.S & LEVAV.J & AVNAIM-PESSO.L. 2011 *Extraneous Factors in Judicial Decisions. National Academy of Science.*

DUNNING. D (2012) *Self-insight: Roadblocks and Detours on the Path to Knowing Thyself.Psychology Press*

DUNNING. D (2011). "The Dunning–Kruger Effect: On Being Ignorant of One's Own Ignorance". Advances in Experimental Social Psychology. pp. 247–296.

EDGER.C (2012) *Effective multi-unit leadership.* Surrey: Gower publishing limited.

FINE.C (2007) *A Mind of its Own: How Your Brain Distorts and Deceives.* Icon Books Ltd.

FINE.C (2017) *Testosterone Rex.* New York: W.W Norton.

FOLKMAN.J (2013) *Exceptional Leaders: Are They the Friend or the enemy?* Forbes

GALLBRAITH.JK (1991) *A history of Economics. The past as the present.* Penguin Economics.

GARVIN.D (2013) *How google sold its engineers on management.* Harvard Business Review.

GLADWELL.M (2005) *Blink: The power of Thinking Without Thinking.* New York: Little Brown and Company.

GAVETT.G (2014) *The Power of Reflection at Work. Harvard Business review.*

GROSZ.S (2014) *The examined life. How we find and lose ourselves.* London: Vintage.

GRUENFELD.D & MAGEE.J & INESI.M.E & GALINSKY.A (2008) *Power and the Objectification of Social Targets. Journal of Personality and Social Psychology. 95 (1) 111-27*

HARDINGHAM.A & BREARLEY.M & VENTER.B & MOORHOUSE.A (2004) *The Coach's Coach: Personal Development for Personal Developers.* CIPD - Kogan Page.

HARRIS.C (2016) *Jaws In Space. Powerful Pitching for Film and TV.* Creative Essentials.

KELMAN.S & HONG.S (2012) *Hard, Soft or Tough Love. What kind of Organizational Culture Promotes Successful Performance in Cross Organizational Collaborations.* Harvard Kennedy School Faculty Research Working Paper Series RWP.

KRUGER, J & DUNNING, D (1999). *"Unskilled and Unaware of It: How Difficulties in Recognizing One's Own Incompetence Lead to Inflated Self-Assessments". Journal of Personality and Social Psychology. 77 (6): 1121–1134.*

JACK.A & DAWSON.A & BEGANY.K & LECKIE.R & BARRY.K & CICCIA.A & SNYDER.A. (2012) *fMRI Reveals Reciprocal Inhibition Between Social and Physical Cognitive Domains. Neuroimage*

JOHN.O & SRIVASTAVA.S (2001) *The Big-Five Trait Taxonomy: History, Measurement and Theoretical Perspectives.* Handbook of Personality: Theory and Research 2nd ed. New York: Guilford.

KAHNEMAN.D (2011) *Thinking Fast and Slow.* New York: Farrar Straus and Giroux.

KAPLAN.K (2009) *Unmasking the imposter. Nature 459, 468-469*

KEGAN.R & LAHEY.L.L (2009) *Immunity to Change.* Harvard Business Review Press.

LALLY. P & JAARDVELD.V & POTTS.CHM & WARDLE.J (2010) *How are Habits Formed? UCL Discovery*

LAURSEN.L (2008) *No you're not an imposter. Science 15th Feb*

LAZARUS.J (2010) *Successful for the results you want.* Surrey: Crimson

LENCIONI.J.B (2002) *The Five Dysfunctions of a Team.* John Wiley & Sons.

MALTZ.M (2015) *Psycho – Cybernetics.* Perigee Books.

MAYER.D (2015) *Setting the Table.* New York: Harper Collins.

McELWEE R.O & YURAK. T.J (In Press) *The phenomenology of the imposter phenome. Individual differences research.*

MEGGINSON.D & CLUTTERBUCK.D (2011) *Techniques for coaching and mentoring.* Oxford: Elsevier.

NEFFINGER.J & KOHUT.M (2014) *Compelling People: The Hidden Qualities That make us Influential.* Piatkus.

OLESON.K.C & POEHLMANN.K.M & YOST.J.H *Subjective Overachievement: individual differences in self-doubt and concern with performance. Journal of personality 68, 491-524.*

PATTERSON.K & GRENNY.J & McMILLAN. R & SWITZLER.A (2011) *Crucial Convocations Tools for Talking When Stakes Are High.* McGraw-Hill Education.

PENNYCOCK G & RAND DG (2019) *Cognitive Reflection and the 2016 Presidential Election. Personality and Social Psychology*

PETERS.S (2012) *The mind management programme for confidence success and happiness.* London: Vermillion

PINKER.S *The Sexual Paradox.* New York: Scribner.

ROCK.D (2009) *Your brain at work.* New York: Harper Collins Publishing.

ROCK.D (2006) *Quiet Leadership.* New York: Harper Collins Publishing.

RONSON.J (2012) The *Psychopath Test.* Picador.

SCOTT.S (2011) *Fierce conversations.* New York: Berkly publishing

SONNAK.C & TOWELL.T *The imposter phenomenon in British university students, relationships between self-esteem and mental health, parenting rearing style and socioeconomic status. Personality and individual differences 31, 863-874.*

SONNERFELD.J (2002) *What makes great boards great. Harvard business review.*

WHITMORE.J (2011) *Coaching for Performance.* London: Nicholas Brealey

WISEMAN.L (2015) *Multipliers: How the Best Leaders Make Everyone Smarter.* HarperBusiness.

WOJCISZKE.B & BAZINSKA.R (1998) *On the dominance of moral Categories in Impression Formation Personality and Social Psychology Bulletin.*

YOUNG.V (2011) *The Secret Thoughts Of Successful Women.* Crown Publishing Group Division Of Random House Inc.

ZAK.P (2013) *The Moral Molecule: the new science of what makes us good or evil.* Corgi.